DEVELOPING EFFECTIVE

INFORMATION SECURITY STRATEGIES

WITH DATA PROTECTION & PRIVACY INSIGHTS

"A GUIDE FOR SENIOR LEADERS & THOSE ASPIRING TO BE"

Dan LoPresto

DEVELOPING EFFECTIVE INFORMATION SECURITY STRATEGIES WITH DATA PROTECTION & PRIVACY INSIGHTS

by Dan LoPresto

Published by Majestic Multimedia Company
P.O. Box 570878 Orlando, FL 32857
info@majestic4us.com

ISBN-13: 978-0-9965332-5-6
ISBN-10: 0-9965332-5-7

Printed in the United States of America
Published on November 9, 2017

DEDICATION

I dedicate this book to my family, friends, peers, and anyone who takes the time to read it…

CONTENTS

PREFACE

In the beginning, as technological advances put computers in our places of business and eventually in our homes, as well as, on our laps, hackers were regarded as tech-savvy wizards who knew their way around these complex machines. Over time, as innovation and advances reached further into our lives, the term hacker took on a new, more sinister, meaning evolving from curious and mischievous to criminal and damaging.

This book serves as an instructive reference for both novice and, most notably, seasoned Information Security leaders facing an unending array of new challenges, threats from all sides, and difficulties demonstrating the value security brings to the organization, along with protecting its brand.

1

The Fundamentals of Information Security

Before computers became personal, portable, and the backbone of nearly every organization worldwide, risks surrounding intellectual property, trade secrets, and other enterprise, as well as personal, information were few. Instead, thieves targeted physical records and equipment.

There were no phishing schemes, very few viruses, and infrequent data breaches. The term **hacker** was reserved for computer-savvy individuals, often sought out for their technical knowledge, expertise, and problem-solving skills. If someone called you a *hacker*, you would have likely considered it a compliment.

Fast-forward a decade or so, and the term hacker took on a whole new context. Hackers were no longer just smart and clever techies, they were tinkerers, testers, and limit-pushers. Fueled by curiosity, challenge, and a "how far can I get" mind-set, hackers enjoyed cracking passwords, accessing "secure" systems, and sharing their accomplishments with like-minded peers.

Soon, virus-writers emerged, along with the thrill and profitability of selling secrets and taking down competitors. Organized crime started to include hacking in its arsenal and found new ways to attack, extort, and steal from a distance.

Malware entered the scene, as custom code allowed nation states, individuals, and practically everyone in-between to infiltrate networked computers, steal data in unprecedented volumes, and sell that information on the global black market.

Attack rates increased dramatically, forcing companies to re-evaluate the ways they handle and mitigate risk. As companies realized that threats to their market share, financial success, and continued existence has increased exponentially and that organizations of all sizes were vulnerable, the role of Information Security Manager formed.

Often residing within Information Technology (IT), the Information Security team's mission resembled that of loss prevention and physical security, yet sought to fortify the organization's infrastructure, networks, endpoints,

and associates via policies, procedures, technologies, and awareness training. The strategic Information Security senior manager quickly earned their seat amidst high-level managers, and eventually executives, discussing everything from risk to return on investment, while building security into the core of every process and position.

Amplifying the voice, tone, and influence of Information Security didn't occur overnight. News of big-name corporations suffering through data breaches, brand erosion, and sinking stock prices slowly, yet surely, turned the heads of C-Level executives toward forming, funding, and further supporting Information Security departments.

Seeking out strong leaders with strategic vision, an understanding of the business, and answers to tough questions, such as how to prevent successful attacks and fortify their networks, where to add "point" solutions to address unique threat vectors, how to increase perimeter security and create "defense-in-depth" solutions and, eventually, how to increase employee awareness while fettering out internal offenders, quickly emerged.

Company executives finally started to recognize a 360° threat landscape and began placing faith in their Information Security management to map out methods to mitigate risk in all directions.

Soon, Information Security managers found themselves with new titles as their teams grew in size and skills, while the importance of their roles expanded. The Information Security manager became senior manager or director and finally donned the title of chief security officer (CSO) or chief information security officer (CISO).

Once this C-Level role matured, Information Security comfortably sat, and continues to sit, at the big table where enterprise-wide strategic decisions are crafted, refined, and minted, while the business forges ahead to strengthen its brand, market share, and its products, services, and solutions.

Throughout recent years, the Information Security discipline has expanded in both depth and width. Information Security senior managers and their teams focus on a wide array of tasks and projects, including: data loss prevention, virus and malware detection and prevention, incident handling, web content filtering, associate awareness, network/application/database security, firewall administration, encryption technologies, risk management, data classification, information assurance, access management, software hardening, business continuity and disaster recovery planning, cloud security, IT controls and auditing, policy writing and revision and even physical/environmental security.

This list only scratches the surface, however, as strategic leadership, partnerships within the business, and an ample dose of charisma enable the Information Security senior manager to foster healthy and productive relationships throughout the organization, along with a security-conscious workforce.

To this day, where Information Security should report remains in debate. Research on the efficacy of each reporting structure would be interesting to monitor; however, it appears that instead of one ideal reporting structure existing for all or most organizations, it boils down to the unique needs within each enterprise that should reveal where Information Security will function most optimally.

In general, having Information Security report into IT can lead to competing for budget initiatives and an overall weakening of an organization's security posture as IT funding is (re-)allocated to a new sales and marketing system or database, network infrastructure upgrades, or similar.

Arguably, having Information Security report into a Chief Executive, Financial or Operating Officer can lead to a wider-than-acceptable disconnect since these roles often are not as technologically-savvy and look for more tangible returns on investment than Information Security can supply which, again, may lead to a lack of priority placed on important and poignant Information Security initiatives and thus, a weakened security posture.

Placing Information Security reporting into a Chief Risk Officer (CRO), also called a Chief Risk Management Officer (CRMO), on the surface, seems to balance the security and technological reporting structure needed for success, however, many large organization have not procured a CRO or CRMO role and department.

"Historically, CISOs have reported to the Chief Information Officer due to their technology-focused role. However, as the CISO position has evolved, more companies are moving towards shifting CISO reporting lines to the Chief Risk Officer (CRO)" [1]. Therefore, where to place Information Security within an organization should evolve as the organization develops and structures itself.

With new technologies, come new threats keeping the Information Security senior manager on their toes. A dynamic, clever, and open-minded Information Security senior manager will forever find challenges to overcome, risks to reduce, and threats to mitigate. Criminals, fraudsters, and other nefarious individuals will always exist and leverage everything they can to steal information for personal gain.

However, the Information Security discipline has matured to the point where it is indispensable within nearly every organization, thus paving the way for Information Security senior managers to continue securing and protecting organizations against external, as well as internal, threats through innovation, strategic decision-making, and deployment of new technologies and solutions judiciously.

The following chapters examine and explore how to expand the Information Security senior manager role, when and where to apply key tactics and strategies, how to become a trusted partner with various business units, and how to empower associates to assist Information Security in its goals and objectives, maintaining data confidentiality, availability, and integrity, thus strengthening the organization's entire security infrastructure. Also, solutions around information protection and privacy, which are tightly-linked to Information Security, will be addressed.

Summary & Additional Insights

Information Security is an extraordinarily rewarding career that has evolved immensely over the past two decades. Presently, there's negative unemployment, meaning there are more jobs available than qualified candidates to fill them.

Just like there's no reliable, authoritative book on how to be the best parent with tons of books published claiming the contrary, you'll find many books related to information security, cybersecurity, and other iterations of *security* that are still very helpful.

The purpose of this book, or guide, is to assist as you begin or help refine much what you already know while, working in such an exciting, ever-changing field. Even the most-seasoned information or cybersecurity professional will learn, at minimum, tactics, strategies, tips, and/or insights in the pages ahead.

2

Establishing a Foundation for Information Security within the Organization

---

Evolution of Information Security within the Business

Roughly a decade ago, Information Security started to find its way into corporations as a separate discipline. Before that, Information Security was merely a job responsibility of one or two Information Technology (IT) associates. Network Administrators were tasked with keeping the network safe and running smoothly, turning off a few unused services, and occasionally looking through logs if something was amiss.

IT administrators issued each associate their own login credentials and tried to make sure only areas necessary for one's job responsibilities were accessible. That was Information Security "back in the day" as they say.

Over time, we found Information Security often placed under the IT umbrella as an emerging sub-department. Information Security was known for its radical ideas, stories of doom and gloom, and several expensive suggestions to mitigate what otherwise appeared as an unstoppable and malicious wave of mayhem. More recently, the field of Information Security has matured greatly and finally shed its sub-department status.

We no longer find the idea of securing our most precious assets, and the perimeter surrounding, them as questionable and obscure. Organizations now value and recognize the need after witnessing, if not experiencing, what a lack of effective security can yield. Corporations have lost vital customer and associate data, given up market share, watched their brand go from top-tier to forgotten, and have even closed-up shop.

Even more recently, and often still linked to IT in some fashion, Information Security has bulked up and expanded into its own, fully-functional department across many mid-sized and large organizations and is now a vital part of an enterprise's success, including the protection of its brand and reputation, as well as, in some ways, generating revenue.

Information Security is no longer simply focused on installing firewalls and anti-virus. Sophisticated hackers, many of which are considered cybercriminals, are using variations of old tactics, along with many new attack vectors, to pierce into corporations' most sensitive data storage areas to exfiltrate any and all data they can sell or maliciously use. Identity theft is a constantly growing concern for consumers all over the world.

We're bombarded with stories all the time about major retailers, hospitals, and financial institutions, amidst others, experiencing massive data breaches. Big-name companies like Home Depot, Target, Neiman Marcus, eBay, JPMorgan Chase, Wyndham Hotels, Adobe, Living Social, Sony PlayStation Network & Online Entertainment, Zappos, Korea Credit Bureau, Facebook, Apple, Gmail, UbiSoft, America Online (AOL), Gamigo, Yahoo, United Parcel Service (UPS), and Evernote all had substantial data breaches between early 2012 and late 2014, with even more corporations affected in recent years, such as Wendy's, Chipotle, Landry's, Horizon Blue Cross Blue Shield, Madison Square Garden, Verizon Enterprises, Oracle, LinkedIn, DropBox, etcetera, plus several government institutions, like the Internal Revenue Service (IRS) and the National Security Agency (NSA). [2]

Each of these organizations had thousands, if not tens, or even hundreds, of thousands of records, breached; some even reaching into the millions. Far from an exhaustive list, these companies and government institutions represent a mere handful of afflicted organizations with hundreds of others also experiencing the same or similar fate and dozens more to emerge this year and beyond.

Business executives and other leaders are far more informed and concerned now than we've ever seen. The importance of information protection is top of mind for them just as it is for consumers. The confident, strategic Information Security leader recognizes the importance of their role and how vital it is to work with the business to ensure their organization remains profitable and secure.

Understanding and Partnering with Major Business Process Areas

Whether you have just started managing or directing Information Security for an organization, or you have been doing so for a while, if you have not spent time with business unit leaders to learn what they do and what is most important to them, you may be missing the boat when it comes to building strong, strategic, mutually-beneficial partnerships and ensuring that Information Security becomes a part of many, if not all, strategic priorities.

All too often, organizations focus on expanding services, new marketing methods, joint-ventures and other major initiatives without a single thought related to Information

Security. By effectively introducing your team and/or yourself, and therefore Information Security, to other areas of the business, they will begin to better understand what you/your team are responsible for, the importance of involving Information Security, seek your support and guidance, along with, and eventually, your approval.

Start by introducing yourself to key business area leaders. You can easily do this via phone or, even better, by stopping by their offices and catching them when they are not terribly distracted. Let them know you are interested in what they do for the company and ask that they explain their roles and major initiatives to you.

Consider carrying a small notepad with you and taking a few notes on their priority projects, areas that challenge their progress, new initiatives, etc. and let them know you would be most happy to assist in whatever capacity is most appropriate.

While this may seem like small talk and pandering, it's most certainly not and instead must be genuine if you are to build strong relationships and rapport with key business leaders. By jotting down what each major business lead does, their pain points, major initiatives, etc., you're building a matrix of knowledge and strategy that you can and should refer to often as you build strong partnerships.

Additionally, you should follow up with business leaders down the road, which will not only impress them, but further strengthen the bond between Information Security and the business. For example, after learning about a new marketing campaign designed to reach younger, technology-savvy consumers, reach back out to the leader(s) launching this initiative a month or so thereafter, ask how the plan is moving along, and if the Information Security department can assist.

Likely, there are several security aspects within the new marketing campaign that only you will pick up on and can thereby bring to the attention of those leading this initiative.

In addition, use this moment to share a bit about a security project or two you are involved with or some ideas you have to strengthen the organization's security program. You might mention forthcoming security awareness training, a new or revised security newsletter, or other methods designed to raise security consciousness and protect the organization's most valuable data and, of course, its brand. Look for additional opportunities to involve Information Security in business areas where it has not yet found a footing.

For instance, ask if you may listen in on conference calls and attend meetings in person to observe what's going on in the business. Again, take some notes and ensure you understand how the organization makes money, new areas of interest and expansion and areas facing difficulty, such as (new) competition, funding, a dearth in expertise, etc.

Try to avoid sharing your ideas and solutions too early as there are likely many forces at play you've not heard about. Hold back your thoughts toward fixing problem areas and, instead, jot them down for revisiting once you know more about each situation.

If asked for your opinion, cautiously share a thought or two, as appropriate, or simply state you'd like to know a bit more before rendering an opinion. You cannot "un-say" a statement or response, and it's far better to share less thought than over-share and say something that makes you appear naïve or short-sighted.

The goal here is to listen, learn, and introduce a security presence to meetings where it otherwise would be overlooked. You'll have time to contribute, as appropriate, down the road, however y our presence, interest, note-taking, and support while attending these meetings, including conference calls, speak volumes to those leading their respective business areas.

Over time, these business leaders will likely seek your input where you'll find yourself in a much better position to share thoughts and lend support. Of course, some ideas, challenges, new initiatives, etc. warrant analysis and may even garner your concern.

Again, jot notes, and once you know enough about the project, the risks it may bring forth, alternatives, compromises and other facets, you may need to share concern(s) and gently push for change. It's always best to have an alternative solution available than to simply highlight a problem area or risk.

Work diligently to avoid being the "negative voice of security" or the department of "no, we simply cannot do that." If a business unit leader demands access to records that, in tandem to the data they need, contain credit card numbers, for example, design a process that can deliver the data this leader seeks without credit card numbers included instead of simply saying "I'm sorry, you cannot have access to this data because it contains credit card numbers belonging to our customers."

Perhaps receiving only the last 4 digits of a credit card number, while the others are masked, would prove more appropriate. In most cases, some form of a work-around or compromise can be reached which maintains the integrity of the security controls designed to protect data. Ensure you have a well-thought-out solution or alternative before you "tell" the business they cannot move forward with one aspect of or an entire project.

Whether it involves marketing via text messaging, where confidential information may inappropriately flow in an unsecured manner or a lack of customer consent may violate a law or regulation within the US or abroad, simply declaring the business must find another way is far from enough.

You may not have a solution at that moment, yet you can frame your response in a more open and understanding manner while still emphasizing other methods are needed. You cannot be expected to know all facets of laws across the globe; however, you can simply suggest that, before marketing to a particular region, the appropriate department research and share any current restrictions.

Another example, along the same lines, might involve requiring encryption for certain data types sent via e-mail. Rather than say "we cannot allow customer account information to be sent via unencrypted e-mail", try another approach…"in order to protect our customer's account information, we ought to establish a more secure method of sending/receiving it, such as encryption within e-mail or Secure File Transfer Protocol (SFTP).

It's often best to steer clear of your initial, "heck no" tendency to respond and instead present alternatives that enable the business to proceed with its initiatives in a far more secure fashion. Few business leaders will accept being told they cannot do something and will likely partner with other departments and/or executives to push back against Information Security's suggestion, or mandate, not to proceed.

Instead, become the secure solutions department, and the business will look to you for guidance and approval as the Information Security discipline in your organization matures and grows. Also, avoid adopting the attitude of "well, if they don't take my advice, it's their problem."

Frankly, that is one way to find yourself seeking a new role elsewhere. Information Security involves much more than securing systems and raising awareness. Information Security leaders recognize that working in harmony with the business helps ensure security-related initiatives are successful.

Why bother to get involved with the business when you have an Information Security department to run? Simply put, just as your input and support will help the business become or remain profitable, assist with exploring new territory, and fix business-related issues, over time, your ideas, efforts, projects, and similar will reveal value and garner appreciation.

Thereafter, you will share *your* goals, initiatives, and the like with key business leaders, invite them to attend *your* meetings and conference calls, when appropriate, and request their feedback and support. Involve these same key business leaders in the solutions to security-related problems and share the credit for success, even if they had a minor role in assisting you.

Appreciation goes a long way and will lead to stronger support bonds between you and the business. When you need funding, cooperation or (additional) backing, these same business leaders, whom you've gone out of your way to help, should be there for you. Keep the cycle going, whereby you lend your support and occasionally solicit theirs.

As long as you remain sincere, versus building a *this-for-that* type relationship, you'll broaden your reach and strengthen your influence while bonding closer with the organization's core. Such partnership may also lead to larger raises, bonuses, and potentially promotions.

You want to reach the point where, as new projects spin up, major players in the business request and value your involvement. In essence, security is as much about securing and protecting the business as it is about relationship-building since the latter helps achieve the former.

Continue Networking with Business Peers In and Out of the Office

All too often, we treat our position as one that begins when we arrive and pauses when we leave for the day; only to resume when we return. In some cases, that may work well in the short or mid-term. Yet, if you are able to network with the business outside of business hours, such as during a sporting event, whether spectating or participating, during happy hour, at lunch or a fundraiser, take advantage of these opportunities to continue building partnerships.

For instance, if your organization has a baseball or bowling league, you can show support by simply showing up and cheer for your co-workers. If you enjoy the sport and can commit the time, consider joining the team. Or, if a particular group goes for happy hour every so often, join them if invited.

Likewise, if you just happened to find yourself at the same establishment during happy hour, stop by and say hello. You may end up invited to the next and subsequent get-togethers. A lot of "shop-talk" occurs outside the office, and you may learn what "lies beneath the surface" of certain projects and other key bits of information not shared in meetings and on conference calls.

Consider this scenario, you're at an offsite company engagement, be it for teambuilding, leadership training, or for any other reason, and are seated near several high-level leaders while one well-respected, yet often quite bold, senior leader shares how she and her team struggle to communicate effectively via only telephone and e-mail

and how instant messaging is used by so many profitable organizations.

Meanwhile, you've fought against the implementation of instant messaging for years as it's a way for proprietary files and information to quickly flow outside the company unbeknownst to Information Security. You/your team keeps a watchful eye on and restricts other communication mediums via a gateway e-mail filter, web content filter, and endpoint protection for portable media.

As the senior leader continues sharing her frustrations, she looks at you and says "...and Security (meaning Information Security) continues to hold us back in the stone age impeding our efficiency with their ban on instant messaging...." You're a bit jarred after this statement, amongst many of your peers. What do you do?

Sure, you can posture-up and preach to her and others about all the risks that you try to minimize and how the business never appreciates the efforts of Information Security. And, you can continue to strongly oppose instant messaging, recalling that you have several (other) supporters in the business, like Risk Management and the Law department. Still, this outside-the-office conversation opened-up an opportunity for you.

Instead of shooting back and adding fire to the existing flames stoked by the senior leader who wants instant messaging, simply consider saying something like "You bring up a very valid point, (name of senior leader). Our goal is not to stifle, control, or minimize communication. We're seeking to enable the safest and most secure means of communication. Let me do some research and see what we can potentially do with Instant Messaging."

You've not promised anything but research, yet you also let her know that you're not close-minded and recognize her concern as a valid one. Then, when you're back at work, chat with your supporters against Instant Messaging, after you do some research on your own, and if possible, you may end up lobbying for Instant Messaging with the right security controls in place.

To expand, within many Instant Messaging configurations, you can enable internal communication only, thereby squelching the risk of external messages and files leaving the organization. In addition, you can turn off file-sharing and have those who need it request access for themselves and their intended, internal recipients for a fixed period of time, based on how long the need access for with a maximum of 6 months or a year.

After that, file-sharing via Instant Messaging is turned off, manually by the team administering it based on a reminder that was created prior, and the individual must request access renewal for another year, or shorter duration, should they need to continue using it.

Once you've researched and selected an Instant Messaging client that can meet the needs of the company, both from a communications and an Information Security perspective, you can garner further support and have now added value to the business, likely not just the senior leader and her team who mentioned they're hurting without it.

You've just avoided being the "my way or the highway" Information Security manager and instead embraced more of a business-supportive, servant leader of Information Security; someone who realizes that there are many ways to make Information Security work with the business rather than against it.
As you continue your conversations with business leaders, you'll gain insight and access to so much more information than would otherwise arrive to you at your desk or simply in the area of the building within which you, and your team if you have one, reside.

All of this information has value as you bond with the business. Look for other opportunities to network with the business. If you're not finding many, consider inviting a few key business leaders to join you at happy hour and be prepared to buy a round of drinks.

Believe it or not, you'll likely end up "in the in-crowd" going forward, which may pave the way to a world of support from business leadership that otherwise would have ignored or appeared too busy to pay attention to security-related projects. While networking with business leaders outside the work walls, you may find the right moment to mention that you're looking into a database monitoring solution to alert and report on fraudulent activity or that the new web content filter has monitoring capabilities that help prevent data loss.

Just as other business leaders will share pain points and ideas, once you're comfortable within this group, the door swings both ways and thus may open up new opportunities to share security-related ideas and challenges.

Establishing Your Team or Managing as an Individual

If you lead a team of Information Security professionals, structuring said team properly can ensure efficient and positive results. If you have any say over how your team is structured, consider a model that best suits the security-related needs of the organization while playing on the individual members' strengths.

For example, if you have two strong technical team members and one less-technical, yet more process-oriented individual, ensure that their titles reflect their responsibilities. Thus, two security analysts and one security project supervisor provides for one simple structure where all three report to a security leader, such as yourself.

Information Security Department

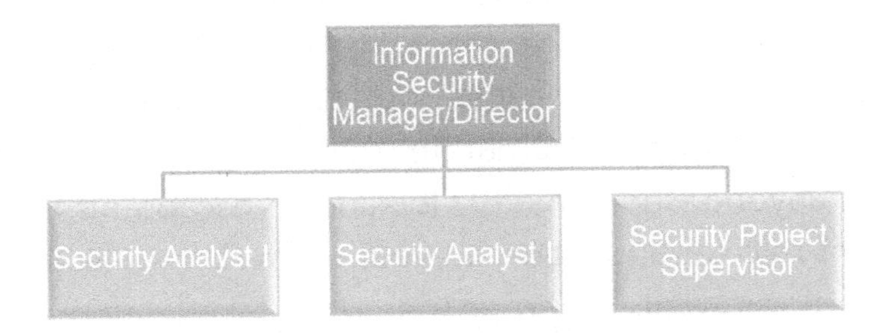

Whether you have one or several reports, seek guidance from your direct supervisor and others, as needed, then form or re-form, your team accordingly. Managing a team effectively has proven a rather dynamic process, and there are tons of books on how to do so. However, in the context of an Information Security team, some key fundaments are vital.

Begin by examining all candidates, internal and external, looking to join your team. Ensure that anyone you're considering hiring has an extremely high-level of integrity and is a rule follower. The organization at large will not appreciate a department who makes and/or enforces, but does not play by, the rules.

For example, if your department reports on employees playing online games while they should be working and thereby refers such cases to Human Resources for disciplinary action, no member of your team should even consider playing online games while in the office. Even if on break, this sends a contrasting and negative message that can destroy your team's credibility.

Second, you need reliable, dedicated team members who are passionate about Information Security. Avoid hiring anyone who is merely looking to escape his or her current role for a position on your team. They'll likely not perform as well as someone who takes Information Security seriously, truly enjoys their work, and makes certain you can depend on them.

Third, while it's not always possible, seek out team members with a strong educational background and, even better, one that involves Information Security or an adjacent discipline, like audit, information technology, anti-fraud, physical security, etc.

If the candidates you end up with do not have a strong, related background, make sure they are open to training and certification down the road. Team credibility is crucial; and classes, training, and certifications that involve Information Security not only help get the job done but also highlight that you and your team are specialists and trusted advisors. Likewise, you will want members of your team to write well, especially when you produce security-related articles and newsletters.

Fourth, yet far from last, you want employees on your team who are excellent communicators as you will rely on them to alert you of potential problems, develop solutions, and explain security concepts and solutions to associates who may be unfamiliar with security, technology, or both.

You'll likely face some challenges while building and managing your team. You may receive pressure, from Human Resources, your boss or others, to hire individuals that already work for the organization versus seeking talent externally. If this happens, you should take their "advice" with a level of caution and ensure that as you interview candidates, they really are a right-fit for the Information Security team you're seeking to build.

Therefore, they must have or be on the verge of acquiring, the education, certifications, and experience needed to do the job. Otherwise, you can certainly try to train them, but that will only go so far as you have other responsibilities, projects to work on, efforts to spearhead, and goals to be reached. If the internal candidate pool lacks the talent you really need, push back, albeit lightly, to those who're promoting the idea of "hiring from within."

Granted, it's great when you have an open position, and an internal candidate has the experience, education, skill set, or some variation thereof that makes them a true fit for the role. If that's not the case, compromising may prove problematic down the road when that individual is tasked with several things to handle and struggles with all or most of them, causing delays on deliverables and potentially frustrating other team members, if not employees, who are impacted by said delays or less-than-adequate results.

Thus, you should, as able, look through the resumes of and perform interviews with both internal and external candidates and choose the best-fit overall. While skills, experience, education, and similar aspects are very necessary in choosing the right candidate(s) to join your team, "fit" in the sense of how good their attitude, organizational and soft skills, (perceived) work ethic, and security-mindset are, cannot be minimized.

In fact, some hiring managers will argue that a candidate's fit with the organization and the team they're looking to join, supersedes their skills, education, and experience. In the end, you need to decide which facets of a candidate hold greater weight than others and recognize that no individual you hire will ever come close to being everything you want them to be.

None of us are perfect...not even you! This is stated to emphasize that many professionals lose sight of the fact that they too need to be flexible, open to constructive feedback, and continue learning, thereby continuously improving themselves.

Even if you don't have a team and are therefore a sole contributor, work with your direct supervisor to ensure that their expectations, along with your major projects, have the necessary resources, such as time and funding. When things seem overwhelming for just you to tackle, look for others outside Information Security, such as a member of the IT staff, and see if their boss will allow them to work on a project with you.

Likewise, always keep your eyes and mind open to taking on new work if you have the resources to do so. For example, if another team manages ID provisioning, see if it would make sense for you (and your team) to take over this process, freeing up the team that presently handles it to work on other areas in need of attention.

The same goes for web content filtering/monitoring, employee investigations, legal holds and other, similar processes that Information Security would have the skill and trust to own and manage. Building strategic business partnerships help weave together security priorities, projects, and achievements.

Whether you have a team or not, it's often too easy to focus on *your* needs, *your* training, *your* certification(s), *your* continuing professional education (CPE) credits and similar. Take time to involve yourself with the needs of your team and/or your peers.

If a team member or co-worker decides to pursue a certification you possess, avoid viewing this as a threat and instead, support them with book recommendations, tips, and knowledge sharing. Encourage members of your team to get certified in security.

There are several certification options, including CompTIA Security+, the (ISC)^2 Certified Information Systems Security Professional (CISSP), the ISACA Certified Information Security Auditor (CISA), and Certified Information Security Manager (CISM), along with the SANS series of Global Information Assurance Certifications, to name a few. While your team members may be following in your footsteps, it's highly unlikely they're vying for or will receive your role, unless you're promoted.

Take pride in the fact that one or several of your team members may follow your lead and decide to get a degree, a certification, or take (additional) training to broaden their knowledge and contribute in a greater capacity. Remember back when you pursued a certification or a degree - were there not others who assisted you? If there weren't, don't you wish someone took an interest in assisting with your success?

Become that individual for those around you, and they'll stick by your side for the long haul. Along those lines, consider reading-up on and learning about "servant leadership." As eloquently stated by author James A. Autry in his book, *The Servant Leader: How to Build a Creative Team, Develop Great Morale, and Improve Bottom-Line Performance*, "Business is of, by, about and for people. And it is ultimately how you are with those people that make all the difference...."

Servant leaders focus not on their accolades, raising their status, and increasing their net worth, but exert equal energy or greater to help all around them become successful and achieve their goals and, by doing so, find their own achievements and successes rising in unison.

In other words, genuinely helping others naturally leads to them helping you and everyone benefitting. Unfortunately, not everyone subscribes to this way of thinking; however, you don't want to be like everyone else. You want to be a true leader and one who is not only successful but appreciated and admired by others.

Managing Your Team, Its Performance, and Yourself

At least once a year, you should assess the team you lead. Examine its strengths, weaknesses, successes, challenges, structure, and alignment with the goals of your direct supervisor and the organization overall.

If you do not have a team, then assess, at least once a year, areas where you could have performed better or more efficiently, such as (on) project deliverables, technology, and process implementations, completing tasks on time, etc. and look for ways to more effectively accomplish your goals. If you delivered (on) a project late, analyze what delayed the effort and make sure to build in "cushions" of time while aiming for completion two to three weeks ahead of schedule, where feasible.

Or, if a new strategy to help reduce risk missed its mark and lacks user support, examine areas where you could have marketed the plan with greater success and garnered stronger sponsorship. Watch for other stumbling blocks that you can address earlier in the process, thus minimizing their potential to derail your efforts.

Starting with your team, presuming you lead one, toward the end of each year, several major assessments should occur. One involves your analysis, and perhaps that of others who work directly with you and your team, as to how well the team did collectively. Through this evaluation, you'll look for both positive and less-than-stellar outcomes and jot down, for your records (at minimum), the pertinent aspects of each.

For instance, if a project that involved rolling out Secure FTP (SFTP) was supposed to be fully functional for all teams by August 1st of this year and now, in December, it's either still not fully implemented or implementation just completed, an analysis of the reasons why this project was not finished on time and which of those reasons involved your team is worth writing down.

If specific members of your team involved with the project dragged their feet, didn't request (your) assistance, neglected to communicate roadblocks, or otherwise strayed from the effort, such details need to appear in their performance evaluation.

Conversely, let's imagine an Information Security Awareness Campaign, with goals that included covering 6 new topics for the company's (online) newsletter by year end, not only led to publication of 6 or more great articles, but additionally received written praise from more than one department on the content "hitting the mark" with employees, this "victory" is one that the entire Information Security department should be proud of and thus recognized for within each individuals', as well as the team's overall, performance evaluation.

Details surrounding this project, such as its on-time completion with well-written, high-quality content and accolades arriving from multiple departments, should appear in each team member's performance evaluation, including yours!

If, either during the performance evaluation process or prior, a team member shares their discontent, either with their performance rating, the way a project went, or some other grievance, or reports an incident, you need to hear their story, document the conversation and, depending on the situation, involve the appropriate individuals and teams to help remedy the problem. For starters, let your boss know unless a complaint involves your direct supervisor.

As an Information Security leader, the tendency to want to solve the issue yourself may arise; however, it's important to get another, objective opinion to help handle the situation your team member raised. Human Resources should assist you in dealing with the issue. They'll help ensure that all the facts come out and that you don't end up in hot water, as you may otherwise have had if you'd sought to take care of the situation yourself.

For example, imagine one member of your team reported to you that they saw another employee stealing equipment. Your employee watched as another employee, on a different team, loaded two monitors into their trunk before leaving the parking lot one evening.

It's great that your employee came to you and reported this, yet if you decided to "take action" and confront the employee who allegedly stole the monitors and, in doing so, learned that they, unbeknownst to you or your employee, were just approved to telecommute and their boss just had them take two company-owned monitors home as part of their home office, you might have an interesting time explaining to your peers and Human Resources that you were trying to handle a situation when, in fact, there really was no situation.

This example, and many other scenarios that could crop up emphasizes the importance of following procedure when it comes to reporting an internal or external incident. The same holds for handling grievances; follow existing procedures.

If none exist, help write them! In the prior example, had you notified Loss Prevention and/or Human Resources prior to confronting and accusing an innocent employee, you wouldn't have to delicately tip-toe through the "why on earth didn't you come to me" conversation the alleged employee's boss may wield at you or the "why didn't you notify our department as our policies and procedures dictate" conversation Loss Prevention or Human Resources might bring up.

Likewise, you wouldn't have embarrassed your boss and possibly your team all because, in the heat of the moment, you acted like a wannabe hero instead of like a strategic leader.

As Information Security professionals, wanting to be the hero is likely a large part of why we do what we do. That said, strategic leaders in our field know when to quell the emotional reaction that bubbles up inside them and think clearly, then react accordingly.

Summary & Additional Insights

The importance of building strong relationships within the organization's business areas cannot be emphasized enough. Likewise, your ability to lead, in a manner more serving toward others, while strategically organizing your team and/or your own efforts will place you on the right paths for success as a leader within Information Security.

Additionally, seeking feedback from your direct supervisor and trusted peers on how you can improve your efforts and effectiveness while helping secure the organization, will lead you toward new paths of success and reward.

3

Weave the Right Security Solutions & Technologies into the Business

Assessing Security Needs via Examination and Risk Identification

While Information Technology governs the overall strategy on which tools and techniques the business needs to succeed, Information Security plays a vital role in most, if not all, business areas and often uncovers issues where: data is less than adequately protected, systems are vulnerable to attack due to a lack of appropriate safeguards, and recently-developed exploits pose a risk to data loss, thus requiring IT to upgrade and/or patch particular applications and systems.

Other examples include examining (aka auditing) and documenting that a new badge system at one or several locations no longer meets Payment Card Industry (PCI) requirements or a sub-department has been sending highly confidential data via e-mail instead of using the organization's encryption solution. This list could go on and on.

As you, the organization's strategic Information Security leader, seek to improve the company's security posture, you must leverage the relationships you've built and continue procuring them as you examine new and existing processes with an eye of scrutiny.

As you come across insecure systems, locate and jot down processes that are not in line with security policies, prioritize your list of findings, and develop well-thought-out plans to address each of them, thus reducing risk. There is a certain level of auditing, often referred to as information security controls, an Information Security leader, and his/her team must take on to be successful since relying strictly on an auditing team to reveal issues may not be enough. If the auditing team is external, they won't initially know the business the way you and your team do.

Hence together, external auditors and the Information Security team (even if by team, it's simply you) will find areas of risk to address, violations of policy, and opportunities for improvement overall. If your organization has an Internal Audit team, though they'll know the business well, you've built relationships across the business, including within IT, and hold additional, keen perspective that can fetter out and correct issues before they impact the brand and cost the company money. Certainly, fixing issues can be costly as well, yet expenses used to fortify the organization are far more acceptable to executive management than money for damage control.

Find Additional Ideas and Solutions Beyond the Office Walls

In your monthly or otherwise occasional meetings with fellow, trusted technology and security professionals outside the organization, ask about and share pain points, solutions and vendors, along with which technologies to embrace and which to avoid. You'll likely learn a lot and help peers while doing so. If you're not already attending local, professional information security-related meetings, add that to your list!

The examples you'll hear from peers may relate to items you're addressing now, or will down the road, as you look for areas to insert necessary security technologies. Conversations with security peers may reveal to you that X vendor, who sells security awareness training, is known for implementation and content problems and that Y vendor, in one or several peers' experience, has terrific and relevant content and smooth implementation at a slightly higher, yet quite worthy, cost than X vendor. Or, you may hear about a new database monitoring tool used to track and monitor associate (user) behavior patterns and alert on abnormalities, such as large percentage increases in record querying and printing.

Had a peer not mentioned this technology, you may not have thought about it as a solution for data leakage and fraud prevention. The value in peer conversations is immeasurable. Of course, you want to ensure what you share about your organization is non-confidential and otherwise generalize how you present certain topics considered company proprietary.

Interview Information Technology Department Leaders & Strategically Assess the Most Appropriate Security Solutions

Back at the office, as you're attending meetings and learning more and more about how the business operates, handles data, etc., you'll certainly find areas requiring Information Security's attention. This is certainly where being analytical and strategic will prove most worthy.

For instance, before requesting or purchasing security technologies to (further) secure your organization, there are several key steps that will ensure you *right-size* security, along with produce a higher return on investment (ROI). If your organization, for example, develops its own web applications, one might assume a web application firewall (WAF) is needed.

While it is certainly possible that a WAF is necessary, it would be most prudent to first ensure that in-house developers are following best practices and standards for creating web applications. Consider meeting with the leader(s) responsible for the web application development team and ask that he, she, or they go over the processes their team follows while writing code.

Once he, she, or they provide(s) a high-level summary of how the team operates, you should ask questions, as appropriate, to learn more and document the answers you receive:

- What quality assurance testing methods are used and when do they occur (at which stages of development)?
- What training courses are taken by developers and at what frequency (annually, twice a year, once every two years, etc.)?
- Are any/all developers following a proven development strategies, such as those found within the Web Application Security Consortium (WASC), Microsoft's Security Development Lifecycle (SDL), and/or the Open Web Application Security Project (OWASP)?

- Is test or actual data used within lower (development) environments?
- Are there, at least, two distinct environments – one for testing and another for production; possibly a third for development, if not coupled with testing?
- How does code move from the testing environment over to production? You're looking for a defined process here.
- Who specifically tests each application?
- Who signs off on each application when it is ready for production?
- (How) Are applications tested once they are released into production? If yes, who tests them – an outside firm or in-house staff or both?

Make certain your "interview" is cordial and reveals a genuine interest in how each area operates. Avoid coming across as an interrogator seeking holes in the process. Granted, you are also looking for process issues, yet that is not the sole reason for this discussion.

This interview, of sorts, is designed to help you continue learning how the business operates, particularly information technology and its surrounding disciplines in this example, as you determine whether or not the organization must acquire a new security solution. Interviewing also establishes information security as an interested, and eventually a governing, party.

In the above example, prior to meeting with the leader(s) responsible for the web application development team, you ought to familiarize yourself with some best practices found within WASC, SDL, and OWASP as to more comfortably understand how secure application development occurs. This will make conversations more fluid and productive.

Post interview, once you have these and similar questions answered, you may come to the conclusion that the organization's web application development team needs to implement several additional controls, such as code checking, documented approvals, better segregation of the testing and production environments, ensuring the person who writes part of or an entire application is not the same person who tests and releases it into production, etc.

You may also determine that very little, or no changes are needed on the development end, however, once applications are released into production, an external firm specializing in web application testing is all that the organization needs. Or, you may conclude to deploy web application firewalls and then run penetration tests against them once or twice annually.

The point here is that learning more about the processes and areas you're looking to protect can reveal substitute or supplementary methods to secure them. All too often, organizations throw security technologies at problems only to realize later, if at all, that the processes themselves need refining and they would have saved a significant sum of money had they first examined and retooled several practices.

Another example may involve installing or replacing an enterprise-wide spam filter, a web content filter, an e-mail encryption solution, or security awareness training. Prior to moving down the path of purchasing a (new) solution that increases security, examine what presently exists, if a solution is indeed in place, by meeting with individuals responsible for each area or technology.

Run reports, as applicable and able, to look for problems with existing systems and/or processes. Share the results with trusted peers within the organization, including your immediate supervisor, and strategically plan, given all the information you've acquired, the appropriate next steps.

If you determine that the enterprise spam filter is not effectively preventing spam from reaching the inboxes of associates, you'll need to first determine how many spam messages hit the filter each day on average and what percentage get through to associates.

Does your enterprise spam filter require an update from the manufacturer versus replacement? Has the organization's e-mail administration team tuned the spam filter since its initial deployment and, if so, how recently have they tweaked it? What filtering rules have been created and tested? Are more rules needed? Are outgoing messages scanned to prevent data leakage?

Messages containing large documents, spreadsheets, databases, and similar formats should be scanned for credit card, social security, and national insurance numbers, the latter of which applies if your organization does business outside the U.S. If messages contain one or several of these types of data, depending on your organization's policy on handling personally identifiable information (PII), they should arrive in a temporary queue for review by Information Security prior to leaving the organization.
Other questions, in this example, include ensuring that all e-mail goes through the enterprise spam filter. While this seems obvious, a misconfiguration in how it was initially set up could reveal that a particular network segment does not route e-mail through the filter or has been completely whitelisted and thus sends and receives unfettered e-mail.

No matter what process or system appears to require stronger security, you should first examine of its current state, generate inquiries through experience, observation, and research, to better understand where attention and change are needed, then decide what else, if anything, must be added to yield the right level of security controls.

Researching Specific Solutions and Working with Vendors

Once you determine a new technology or other solution is required, research top-tier vendors and products and try to eventually narrow your search results down to three. Build a business case that articulates how this technology will benefit the organization. Will it reduce risk? Can you quantify the risk reduction? Will not securing this data leave it vulnerable to compromise, thus costing the company far more money than the security technology you're looking to acquire and implement?

Conversely, you certainly want to avoid purchasing a solution that costs more money than the system(s) and data it's designed to protect. If you have the funding, consider hiring a vendor agnostic solution provider to assist you in selecting three solutions, then schedule introductory meetings with each of the three vendors, offering said solutions, so you can ask questions on how their solution works and will address your organization's needs. Take copious notes and have a list of several key questions to present to each vendor.

Questions may include: Are we required to purchase upgrades and support each year or are they included? Does this solution also cover other areas, such as Unix or Linux-based systems? What types of training on the vendor's solution is available to us and what does that cost? What levels of technical assistance do you offer, when are they available, and do they cost extra?

In addition, ask specific questions related to how the solution protects your organization's systems and data, as well as ways to present return on investment. After going through this process with each vendor, using the questions you prepared and asked about, create a spreadsheet that scores each vendor's answers so you can come up with a number one, two, and three choice.

You may find that the best solution is far more expensive than the next best choice or that the option appearing to be the least expensive has auxiliary costs that force you to pay for upgrades, technical support, and training, thus rendering it more expensive in the end.

Your decision should not be based solely on price; however the cost will likely still compose one major facet of the decision-making process. Also, your compliance or audit department may request copies of your notes to ensure that an objective approach to selecting a vendor was performed.

Such notes, if properly dated and organized, will prove invaluable time and time again. Similarly, an executive in another area may also, months later, want you to explain to a governance board, or similar group, why you chose this particular technology and vendor.

With so much going on between when the decision was made and when you're being asked to share your process, reasons, etc., you'll thank yourself for taking, saving, and organizing notes on each major initiative you work on.

Lastly, once a vendor is selected, a process to review their contract and related documents, like their terms of service, privacy policy, statement of work (SOW), etc. by all relative business partners, such as those responsible for Internal Audit, Law, Information Technology (IT), Insurance/Risk Management, Human Resources (HR), others and, of course, Information Security.

Contract negotiation is vital to ensure you not only get what you pay for, but that terms and liabilities are established to protect each organization, especially the one you work for. Also, non-disclosure agreements (NDAs) help ensure private information remains as such.

Earlier, the term vendor agnostic solution provider was mentioned. These solution providers aim to save you time, in exchange for a fee, researching best-of-breed and other major technology and information solution providers (aka vendors). They also get to know your networks, systems, and overall business to then help select the vendor(s) whose product or service best matches your needs.

Whether you hire a company like this is no substitute for your own research and due diligence. A vendor-agnostic solution provider, at best, should become a strong supplement to your examination of what's available.

Hence, you may partner with a vendor agnostic solution provider and together select what's best for the organization. This helps lend credence to the decision to purchase X vendor's solution since another company, in tandem to your organization's Information Security leader, selected it.

After purchasing a security technology, or during contract negotiation, if offered by the vendor, consider having them implement the solution versus having your organization's staff handle installation and configuration. Unless your in-house staff has a lot of experience in this area, a partnership with the vendor will help ensure implementation goes smoothly and the solution (aka application, appliance, system) gets configured correctly.

A joint effort, between in-house IT staff and that vendor, might also prove a viable option. Otherwise, a less than perfect installation can lead to embarrassment while executives potentially lose faith in the solution you picked.

Also, a misconfigured solution may leave a gaping hole that exploits a different system or the very one you're trying to protect. Don't let the added cost of professional, vendor-driven implementation of a new security solution dissuade you, particularly if in-house IT staff are uncomfortable or otherwise lack expertise in this particular area.

If you have, or can acquire, subscription access to a global research and advisory firm, like Forrester, Gartner, or Info-Tech Research Group, with specialization in the area of Information Security, doing so will enhance your research of top-rated vendors, products, and their features, as well as known threats, solutions, advice, and more.

Utilize this research tool, along with professional advisory services, often included, to keep up with security trends, do's and don'ts, etc. Professional advisory services allow you to seek advice from a subject matter expert in such areas as ID provisioning, 2-factor authentication, public and private key encryption, methods to become or remain Payment Card Industry (PCI) compliant, along with any other topics you're focusing on to meet regulatory obligations and company, as well as security, objectives.

While access to these services is not cheap, if used often and correctly, they will prove their worth several fold. It's important to note here that the newest solution on the market may not be the best for your environment.

Hence, subscription access to a global research and advisory firm is one of several tools, coupled with your own research, discussions with peers, and vendor agnostic solution providers that aid in selecting the right security technologies and services for your organization.

You may not have the budget for all of these tools and methods and, if that's the case, select the one or two methods that are most feasible for your organization, given financial constraints. Also, any application, appliance, or solution that claims to "do it all" likely doesn't handle each facet of security it claims to cover, equally well. The saying "there is no killer app" holds true.

On the opposite end of the spectrum, you have "point solutions" that address a unique aspect of security. In some cases, that is all you need. More often though, it's best to get a solution that meets several security needs at once.

Thus, you end up somewhere in-between a point solution and the infamous killer app. Hopefully, the security solution(s) you select for the business, where appropriate, can interconnect and thus work well with existing systems for, at a minimum, the purposes of reporting, metrics, and testing.

Technologies that "play well together" yield far fewer headaches down the road. Still, every system may not integrate fully and, if a solution you desperately need won't work with one or two of several dozens of other systems, you're likely still in good shape.

Don't forget to update, or have the appropriate individual(s) revise, training materials, policies, procedures, network and infrastructure diagrams, and other documentation to reflect newly implemented security systems. This includes creating custom, technology training manuals derived from materials the vendor supplies, along with the specific procedures the team(s) responsible follow.

It's important to document and/or export the settings and configurations of the new security system so that if it needs to be replaced, you're not setting it up from scratch. Auditors appreciate such documentation as well.

Conducting Your Own Risk Assessments

If you have not already done so, or it has been a while, conduct a risk assessment of the entire enterprise, one area at a time. If another team already performs this function, meet with them to go over results and ask how you can become involved with their next risk assessment, even if only to observe and take notes.

You can conduct periodic, informal risk assessments as well and focus on particular business areas if that method fits the needs of the organization best. The idea here is to continue your quest to look for weaknesses in the business and where confidential data may be stolen, fraud may occur, hackers may exploit, etc. Begin by inventorying all systems and applications in a spreadsheet. Consider a style like that depicted here.

Risk Assessment - Summary Report

System or Application	Risk Rating**	Risk Assessment Responsibility		Review Dates		Business Impact Ratings *			Next Step ****	General Comments	Info Security Leader Comments
		Manager	Location	Date of This Review	Next Review	Confidentiality	Integrity	***Availability / Critical Time Scale			

*Business Impact Ratings:
A - Probable
B - Highly Possible
C - Possible
D - Unlikely
E - Very Unlikely

**Risk Rating:
L - Low
M - Medium
H - High

***Availability Critical Time Scales:
1 - An hour
2 - A day
3 - 2-3 days
4 - A week
5 - A month

****Next Step:
Low risk - Complete with this process.

Medium and High - complete in-depth risk assessment.

Determine Next Review Date.

Approvals: I agree with the security analysis defined above.

Business Manager ________________ Date __________

Information Security Leader ________________ Date __________

Company Confidential

You'll want to review policies as part of your risk assessment; also procedures, along with new and older technologies -- are they configured correctly and optimally given changes in the infrastructure applied over time? In addition, examine resourcing -- is there a very understaffed department causing important checks and balances to be missed?

The organization's culture may be one that promotes trust between associates, which is a great thing, yet if it's too trusting, and associates don't feel the need to lock their workstations when they step away, the risk of a curious or upset associate accessing information they are not privy to, leaking confidential data, or sabotaging a system exists and needs to be dealt with. Hence, organizational culture plays a role in your risk assessments.

Rate the vulnerabilities and areas of concern in order of most likely to cause a (serious) issue to least likely, then determine what solutions you and other associates in the business can apply to mitigate the risks. Research online, as well as via speaking with peers in and outside your organization, to help pull together risk assessment criteria if you don't already have a documented methodology. Some basic risk assessment terminology you may find useful is shown here.

Term	Definition	Example
Risk	**WHAT** can happen if the threat exploits a vulnerability. The potential for an undesirable event.	Corrupted data resulting in quality of service issues, potential lawsuit.
Vulnerability	**HOW** a weakness in technology or organizational process could be exploited by a threat to gain unauthorized access to information or to disrupt processing.	Insufficient training program.
Threat	**WHO** or what can cause an undesirable event. Source of Danger.	Personnel.
Outcome	**OUTCOME**: Disclosure, modification, destruction/loss, interruption **Typical Correlation Between Outcome & Security Requirement**: Disclosure = Confidentiality Modification = Integrity Destruction / Loss = Integrity or Availability Interruption = Availability	Confidentiality = Personally Identifiable, Health or similar highly-confidential information disclosed to an unauthorized associate. Integrity = Personally Identifiable, Health or similar highly-confidential information modified by an unauthorized associate. Availability = System down and highly-confidential information is unavailable to associates.
Probability (Low, Medium, High)	The likelihood that an event will occur.	Low = 1, Medium = 2, High = 3
Impact (Low, Medium, High)	The effect on an organization's mission and business objective.	Low = 1, Medium = 2, High = 3
Risk Score	This will be the Total Risk Score based on the Probability and Impact. This score is calculated by multiplying the Probability and the Impact together. The highest score possible would be a 9.	A Probability of a 2 and an Impact of a 3 results in a score of 6.

Summary & Additional Insights

Information Security leaders recognize the need to assess and address the security needs of an organization via process and system examination, research, conversations with peers, interviews with business associates, analysis, partnerships and risk assessments.

Asking key questions, taking and saving lots of notes, and working with business associates while contracting with vendors are all necessary components to effectively secure your organization using appropriate security solutions and technologies. As you continue to follow these methods, you'll develop several of your own as you help fortify your organization's security posture.

4

Build and/or Review and Revise Information Security Policies

Arguably, the foundation of security within an organization rests within its policies. Without policies, associates lack written guidance differentiating between acceptable and prohibited behavior. Procedures, standards, guidelines, and similar documents should all relate back to high-level, executive-supported policies.

In most cases, a policy applies to every associate within the organization. In some cases, however, a policy may have sections that apply only to certain segments of the workforce, such as part-time, non-exempt, or exempt associates, etc.

As long as they are well-written and periodically reviewed and approved by the governing executive bodies within the organization, your policies will successfully guide behavior and otherwise support a disciplinary action for those electing not to follow them. For the strategic Information Security leader, a focus on strong, effective information security and related policies is a key factor to running a successful department and securing the organization.

The following is not meant to be an exhaustive list, but instead a starting point for your organization. Each organization should create a list of policies that uniquely addresses its needs. Here are a few that relate to information security with suggested content areas:

I. Policy A – Information Security
   A. General data protection and usage
      1. Labelling of confidential and sensitive documents / materials
      2. How to report instances where confidential or sensitive data has been left unsecured
   B. Appropriate data handling & storage
      1. Encryption requirements
      2. Areas where certain types of data may not be stored
      3. Methods where certain types of data may not be transmitted
   C. Access provisioning / de-provisioning
   D. Data access rights per job role
   E. Handling associate terminations

II. Policy B – Physical Security

A. Access badges

1. Visitor / Guest, Contractor, Employee
2. Lost Badges
3. Re-badging (changes to existing)
4. Badge reclaiming (upon a move or leave)

B. Facilities security

1. Locked doors and cabinets to secure documents and other valuables
   a) *Issuing, tracking, & reclaiming keys*
   b) *Reporting unlocked doors, broken locks, etc.*
2. Security cameras / Closed Caption Television (CCTV)

C. Security Guards & Loss Prevention staff

D. Laptop & Desktop Computer locking cables

E. Physical Security reports

F. Other Security devices

III. Policy C – Data Privacy

A. General classifications of data

1. Public (Basic Risk)
2. Company Confidential (Medium – High Risk)
3. Sensitive / Restricted (High Risk)

B. Simple Data Classification Matrix

C. Data Loss Prevention (DLP) scans

1. Run X times per year (quarterly or twice annually)
2. Scan Desktop & Laptop computers, also Network Shares and Cloud storage for high-risk data items stored in an area that violates policy
3. Files in question are quarantined and reviewed
4. File owners are contacted via e-mail with 30 days to respond
5. Reporting & metrics

IV. Policy D - Media Handling & Document Storage

A. Approved media for company-related data

1. Encrypted USB / Thumb Drives issued by IT dept.

2. Encrypted CDs / DVDs

B. Approved data transport mechanisms

1. Secure courier
2. Secure fax
3. Secure e-Mail
4. Encrypted USB / Thumb Drives issued by IT dept.
5. Cloud Storage and Sharing Site(s)
6. Secure File Transfer Protocol (SFTP)
7. Encrypted e-Mail

C. Storage of company confidential and sensitive / restricted documents

1. Approved storage facilities
   a) *Vendor off-site storage*
      (1) Physical locations
      (2) Cloud storage
   b) *On-site secure facilities (rooms, sections of the building...)*
   c) *Company-owned safes*
   d) *Locked drawers and cabinets*
2. Managing access to each protected area
   a) *Keys*
   b) *Access Logs*
   c) *Digital access rights (if stored online)*

V. Policy E-Business Continuity & Disaster Recovery Planning (BCP)

A. Responsible departments

B. Each business unit's level of involvement, as appropriate

C. Completion of major Business Continuity & Disaster Recovery tasks

1. Business Continuity & Disaster Recovery Plan review
2. Business Continuity & Disaster Recovery Plan updates
3. Business Continuity & Disaster Recovery Plan testing
4. Business Impact Analysis (BIA)
5. Business Continuity & Disaster Recovery Plan certification
6. Business Continuity & Disaster Recovery Plan approval

D. Maintenance of Call Lists (Trees)

E. Emergency Notification System (ENS)

1. Used to announce an actual Business Continuity & Disaster Recovery event to all first-responders within the organization

2. Used to test response times of first responders periodically each year

3. Kept up-to-date with first-responders from each team that has Business Continuity and/or Disaster Recovery responsibilities

F. Business Continuity & Disaster Recovery intranet page or SharePoint

1. Maintained with updated information

a) *Business Continuity & Disaster Recovery Plan test results*

b) *Links to Call Lists (Trees)*

c) *Relevant articles*

d) *Tools*

2. Reviewed periodically

G. System Backup procedures

1. Cloud backup

2. Tape or other media backup

3. Responsible departments

a) *Reference to written Standard Operating Procedures (SOPs)*

VI. Policy F - Identity Theft Prevention

A. Establishment of Identity Theft Prevention Program

1. Red Flag rules

a) *Warning signs of identity theft triggers during day-to-day operations*

2. Follow Federal Trade Commission (FTC) guidance

B. Identity Theft training for all associates

1. What is Identity Theft

a) *Statistics*

b) *Examples*

2. What are Red Flag rules

3. How to report incidents

VII. Policy G – Business Records Management

A. Define business record types (work with business leaders in each department)

B. Record retention guidelines

1. Local laws may impact how long the organization must retain records

C. Properly storing / securing records

D. Schedule (matrix) of record types versus how long to store / secure each

E. Resources to seek for assistance

VIII. Policy H – Use of Social Media and similar technologies

A. Define Social Media

1. Examples

B. Appropriate vs. inappropriate use of Social Media sites

C. Code of conduct

1. Post accurate, non-proprietary information
2. Peer review of planned postings
3. Select proper images (photos, graphics, etc.)
4. Protect the brand

D. How to report misuse or negatively-impacting Social Media posts

E. Potential disciplinary action for defamatory, inaccurate or other detrimental postings

Each policy, if placed on the organization's intranet or internal SharePoint, should link to related polices, standards, etc. to provide associates with more context, further examples, etc.

You need not write each and every one of the aforementioned policies, however, your input, review and relevant examples should help develop and evolve them.

Thereafter, each policy receives further review from Human Resources (HR), Information Technology (IT), and other appropriate departments, including executive management, who will provide final sign-off and approval.

If policies, like those above, already exist, they must undergo review on an annual basis. Lead the charge and recruit other department managers to review and offer input on these policies. All too often, key elements are missing, yet can be inserted during such reviews, strengthening the policies and, thus, the information they convey. Likewise, new technologies, threats, risks, and similar emerge constantly, some of which may need to be referenced within said policies.

Conversely, you may find the need for new policy creation over time as the business, along with the technologies surrounding it, change. If a policy gets too large, cumbersome or confusing, it may prove best to create two similar, yet distinct policies to cover the areas formerly housed.

If you find the content within Information Security-related policies becoming too specific, consider re-planting the more detailed information into a procedure or standard. Polices are intended to provide general guidelines, while procedures and standards get into the nitty-gritty.

If you create related procedures and/or standards, and all appear online within the organization's intranet or SharePoint, make sure they link together appropriately as some associates will need to efficiently move from reading a policy into reading its related standard(s) or procedure(s) to get the answers they seek and ensure their actions are compliant.

Some challenges all information security leaders face include associates simply ignoring company policies and choosing instead to behave in a manner that best suits their agendas regardless of the (potential) impact it may have on the organization. A survey taken several years ago revealed that "of 165,000 workers, nine out of ten knowingly ignore or violate data (cyber safety) policies." [3]

Despite being warned of the risks, employees routinely share their passwords, jot them down on post-it notes or similar, and engage in other insecure practices. With an average of 90% of employees knowingly violating security-related policies, compliance certainly seems an uphill battle, however, consider the fact that policies without "teeth" (aka strong consequences) are regarded as mere suggestions.

Hence, partner with your HR department to add consequences of not following policies within actual policy language. Phrases like, "Failure to follow company policies may result in disciplinary action, up to and including termination." Then, make sure HR will indeed stick to their guns if, or when, violations occur.

Once one or several employees are disciplined for ignoring or otherwise violating company policies, word will spread amongst the workforce that organizational policies are indeed strictly-enforced. It often comes down to the carrot versus the stick in situations like this, where employees are either motivated to follow policies positively or fearful of the consequences of not following them.

You can, in addition to helping establish consequences for not complying with policy, establish reward for unique situations where, by following company policy, an employee or several thwarted an attack or saved the company money. Such accolades and rewards should only be given out when there is a significant, positive result that occurs based on good behavior and aligns directly with policy mandates.

It's fruitless to frequently reward associates for doing what's expected. Doing so only builds a culture of "if they reward me, I'll do the right thing." Instead, those who go way above and beyond should be recognized for doing so, which may, in turn, inspire others to do the same.

Lastly, make certain that your annual Information Security awareness training, along with any other related training materials, such as posters, e-mails, newsletters, and similar, reference related policies, procedures, and standards while encouraging associates to familiarize themselves with them. A compliant workforce can make all the difference between becoming a victim and thwarting a social engineering attack, for example.

If the workforce understands the types of threats they may encounter, recognizes red flags (identity theft warning signs), knows how to react during a business continuity crisis, understands what is and isn't appropriate to post on social media and how to report concerns, grasps how to protect business records and properly handle company documentation and media.

As well as, with what to do when physical aspects of security break down, you and your department, and the organization at large, will be well-armed against the myriad of problems that seriously impact many other organizations. Watch for additional opportunities to train and empower the workforce to embrace information security and related best practices.

Summary & Additional Insights

Policies, standards, guidelines, and similar documents, related to Information Security and adjacent disciplines, represent a strong, reliable foundation and serve as a source of reference and requirements for all associates.

Policies, in particular, must include consequences for failing to follow them.

All documents, serving as policies, benchmarks, guidance, etc. should be distributed and/or made easily available to all associates; appearing prominently within the organization's intranet or similar space, for example.

Associates without access to online resources need to receive paper copies of relevant documents. Certain internal documents, such as data protection, network access, and non-compete agreements, must be signed by associates and logged appropriately within Human Resources.

Policies, standards, and guidelines should be reviewed annually, and updated by subject matter experts, then signed-off on by the owner(s); usually executives within the organization. If/when any of these documents, notably internal agreements, are significantly changed, a process requiring all associates to re-review and sign them should commence.

5

Partner with, Guide, & Empower Users

Turn Users' Lack of Awareness into a Fortified Training and Communications Program

A common phrase touted by Information Security professionals takes on one form or another of the following: "the weakest security link in any organization is its user base." While this may prove true in many organizations, it most certainly doesn't have to.

In fact, if the company you work for has a weak user (aka associate or employee) base with regard to security, turn this issue into an opportunity and strengthen the workforce's knowledge, understanding, and appreciation of information security.

For starters, assess whether or not associates understand the fundamentals of information security. Look under keyboards, on sticky notes on and around associate desks and in related areas for posted passwords. Ask random associates across multiple departments a few basic questions, when the opportunity arises, about security both in the workplace and at home.

Notice if associates walk away from their desks without locking their computers. While you likely have a computer policy that automatically locks workstations after 15 minutes of inactivity, a simple movement of the mouse or stroke of a key, by someone up to no good, resets the 15-minute timer and can enable them to swing back around and access information they are not privy to.

After surveying whether or not your organization's associates exhibit bad security posture, put together a list of areas to address, such as password security, locking workstations when leaving one's desk, shoulder surfing awareness (which involves looking out for associates who peek over your shoulder to see what you're typing in for your password, etc.), putting away confidential documents and locking desk and cabinet drawers before leaving (clean desk policy), removing confidential faxes and printouts from machines quickly after their received/printed, etc.

Next, assess whether these topics, amidst many others, appear in your (annual) security awareness training. If your security awareness training was purchased and therefore cannot be altered with your own content, consider "quick hit" training that can be delivered via your learning management system (LMS) or possibly via an intranet or SharePoint page.

Also, use topics, or "issues," you uncovered, amidst others you've experienced in the past or find via research, to help form a monthly or quarterly newsletter that shares valuable tips, tricks, dos and don'ts, best practices, and similar that help associates stay secure in the office and at home. The newsletter can be digital or printed; possibly both as there may be associates who have limited access to computers as part of their jobs.

Regardless, users will appreciate a newsletter they can read while at home, on break, or wherever they are, provided it's relevant, interesting, and informative. Partner with peers in Information Technology (IT) and Human Resources (HR), for example, to author articles on particular information security topics of interest, including phishing, securing confidential documents, encryption, e-mail and browser safety, social engineering, ransomware, and other related subjects. Such articles can be shared several times a year to raise security awareness and promote healthy computing.

Consider having an e-mail sent to all associates, from the company's communications or a related department, containing a short title and blurb with a link to the full article posted on the company's intranet or SharePoint. Interested associates will then click on the link to read the full article, often finding useful information for home computing weaved in. Request that managers highlight these articles during team meetings and encourage their direct reports to read them.

Remember, you need not author all articles. Your peers in IT and other areas can, and should, assist. Short meetings with your peer article authors roughly once a month should keep everyone on track, sharing ideas and producing quality, informative articles written for a general audience.

Steer clear of overly-technical material and define all your acronyms upon their first appearance within articles. Once you and your peers have written half a dozen or more articles, you can reuse them each year after reviewing and updating them accordingly, possibly adding or removing some examples as appropriate.

Create Security Rewards and Stewards

Also, consider developing a "security rewards" program whereby associates who go above and beyond in handling a security-related situation, such as noticing a social engineering call and documenting all they can about the caller, then reporting it to the Information Security department, result in the astute associate receiving a $20 gift certificate to a local restaurant, retailer, or online shopping site.

A small budget for these rewards will go a long way toward empowering associates to keep a watchful eye for fraud, social engineering, and other malfeasance that could otherwise lead to a data breach causing harm to the company financially and impacting its brand.

You can also create a "Security Steward" program across the enterprise where interested individuals will meet with Information Security, in person or via conference call, during quarterly meetings, for example, to discuss new projects that appear to have some several facets that relate to security or new practices that may have weakened security in a particular area of the business.

For example, a new time and expense system may involve transmitting bank account numbers to an external vendor without encryption. A Security Steward working in that area, empowered to do the right thing for the company, might bring this concern up during a quarterly meeting with Information Security, which launches a research initiative to determine the risks and offers an alternative, more secure data transmission solution.

Evade the Stigma of the Department of "No"

The Information Security department must ensure that it brings forth solutions to issues after ample research and discussion ensues. Never become the departments of "no." In other words, Information Security will not gain respect and valued partnerships with the business if it is regarded as the department that always throws a wrench in the works.

For instance, the business launches a new social networking program to reach out and market to a younger audience and the Information Security department declares "we cannot use social media in this fashion as these potential, younger customers we communicate with may transmit their own personally identifiable information publicly, subjecting themselves to identity theft and us to a liability lawsuit."

Now, while this example may indeed prove risky, not just for younger customers, Information Security should raise the concern – social media may yield public communication of personally identifiable information (PII) – and then, offer a means to prevent such from occurring.

For instance, when we use social media marketing channels, we need to boldly communicate, via a persistent disclaimer, for example, that public correspondence should only contain questions and answers and not involve any PII and as individuals express interest, the communications move to a private mechanism, that being e-mail, phone, or some other one-to-one, non-public medium.

Now, Information Security a has effectively shared a concern and offered a solution. Further, the organization may enable a means to delete, as soon as it locates, public postings that contain personally identifiable information (PII) as to protect the individuals they are marketing to and communicating with. PII consists of data that can be used to identify an individual.

Examples of PII include first and last name, e-mail address, mailing address, driver's license numbers, social security numbers, passport numbers, dates of birth, and similar data. Just as the organization will have a policy around appropriate storage and transmission of PII, it will need procedures to ensure that PII is discouraged on social media and can be removed, if posted publicly, to protect individuals.

Provide Facts and Figures, Not Just Useful and Interesting Information

Whether writing articles, creating posters to place around printers, faxes, and copy machines and in break rooms, designing security awareness training, or holding lunch-n-learns, where you speak on a topic during the lunch hour and interested associates bring lunch and listen in to learn more, make sure you include some statistics, as such adds to the validity of what you're trying to communicate.

The Internet is laden with viable sources for Information Security facts, stats, incidents and more, such as SANS.org, the Verizon Data Breach Report, NIST.gov, Gartner.com, IAPP.org, and ISSA.org.

Incorporate key pieces of articles found at these and similar sites, with proper citation to their source, so that your communications will come across as not only informative but reliable and factual.

One example would be, amidst an article you're putting together on data breaches and risks, you could mention that "according to the Verizon Data Breach Report..., there were 44 million records compromised..." And, you might mention that if 44 million records were reported as compromised, how many million more went unreported? You'd then continue emphasizing your points as to the importance of protecting company and customer records to prevent data compromise.

Don't forget Red Flags Rules (Identity Theft Prevention)

Beyond security awareness and quick hit training, articles, lunch-n-learns and meetings with Security Stewards, your organization, if considered a financial institution or creditor, needs a Red Flags Rules program – which involves the creation and implementation of a written identity theft prevention program, as per the Federal Trade Commission's (FTC) Bureau of Consumer Protection. Even if your organization is not a financial institution or creditor, consider creating an anti-identity theft prevention program anyway.

Simply put, you, along with members of your Compliance, Human Resources, Information Technology, and potentially one or two other departments, would perform a risk assessment to determine where, within day-to-day operations, stolen or fraudulent information could potentially be used to inappropriately open or access an account or otherwise commit some form of identity theft.

Per the FTC, Red Flags are suspicious patterns or practices, or specific activities that indicate the possibility of identity theft. [4] You and the team responsible for creating and implementing the Red Flags Rules program would identify these risky patterns, practices, and activities.

An example of a Red Flag Rule might be that, when sales representatives receive information from a prospective new customer while examining the documentation supplied by the prospective customer, noting that a supplied address does not match any of the addresses within the consumer's existing records. This should trigger further analysis and possible action to prevent a fraudulent account from being opened.

Just as you would test your security awareness program, your identity theft (Red Flags Rules) awareness program should also receive some form of validation that it is effective and that associates know what to do when a suspicious event is detected.

Create an Information Security Strategy & Governance Committee

Many of the aforementioned tasks, methods, and programs, amidst others, belong on the agenda of a committee. You should consider forming such a committee, focused on Information Security & Privacy Strategy, including Governance.

As you form this committee, you'll 'cherry pick' key members from departments you work with, such as Information Technology, Risk/Compliance, Physical Security/Loss Prevention, Finance and Legal, to meet at least quarterly and go over initiatives, programs, projects, and related tasks.

Each member is expected to update the committee on the status of relevant projects, while others share thoughts and opinions as new topics are brought up. The committee would then report their findings, successes, struggling points, progress, etc. to a higher-level manager, such as a Vice President, to whom Information Security reports.

The Information Security & Privacy Strategy and Governance Committee also makes recommendations to upper management, such as "before we merge the databases belonging to two separate projects that are now becoming one larger project, we assess (audit) who currently has access and at what levels, then determine, post merge, those who should retain their rights, along with others who no longer require access to the data therein." By "we", it may be that a member of the Information Security team or an IT Controls Group would perform the audit versus actual members of the committee.

Generally, committee members are in management and may or may not handle technical tasks directly. In other cases, technical managers indeed perform audits, examine access tables, review database structures and rules, etc.

By creating and managing an Information Security & Privacy Strategy and Governance Committee, you open doors to achieving even more synergy with your business partners and together suggest changes, create and work on new projects, and achieve goals that otherwise would be quite difficult for one person, or even department, to handle alone. Meeting agendas and minutes must be filed for reference and can be used to create each subsequent meeting's agenda in order to keep track of action items and their status.

Each of the aforementioned programs, strategies, projects, and similar will help you create more value for the business and thus make a greater impact, while strengthening the organization's defenses against hackers, fraud, identity theft, and similar forms of malfeasance. In addition, you'll accomplish much more, than those who attempt to do the same solo, while forming stronger bonds with the business.

The importance of the latter cannot be emphasized enough. The role of the Information Security leader has changed and evolved, as stated within an SC Magazine article, "As opposed to being security's gatekeeper, the voice that could be counted upon to squelch a plan or strategy perceived as too risky or apt to open up the organization too much, today's CISO (Chief Information Security Officer) is more of a protector and counselor for a company's lines of business." [5] The CISO role continues to evolve, for that matter.

Hence, the business partnerships you'll make and maintain within your organization will ensure that the goals of the business, in tandem to your own, shall be achieved with greater frequency and with more support. Become more than just "the security guy/gal" at your organization and you'll proudly rise to the top of your game!

Summary & Additional Insights

Information Security and Data Protection training and awareness are vital and their importance cannot be over-emphasized. Some creativity in how you deliver awareness to associates will go a long way. An annual, catch-all, online awareness training, while potentially a part of the overall awareness and communications program, will not work by itself.

Successful security and data protection awareness and communications programs offer frequent, poignant content via several channels, and provide associates with guidance and knowledge they will use at work and, in some cases, at home.

Rewarding associates for their astuteness and efforts leading to the thwarting a security-related issue, such as fraud or insider malfeasance, is an inexpensive, yet powerful tool. The more eyes the company has out there looking for noteworthy mistakes and misbehavior; the stronger security posture your organization will achieve.

Information Security is a partner to the business. It is not a roadblock against productivity and efficiency. That said, there are certainly cases where saying "no" is appropriate, yet it should be followed-up (immediately) with "yet, can we try it this way" or some other alternative solution(s) until an effective compromise is reached. Where there's a will…

Use citable statistics, facts, figures, and occasionally quotes from prominent individuals, as appropriate, to supplement your efforts toward the purchase of new security and data protection technologies, for changes to existing (security) architectures, for replacing old, no longer supported/patchable/secure applications and systems, for necessary headcount increase (temporary or permanent), etc. Be prepared to wait on the "go ahead" and strategic, as well as open-minded, in how you accept rejections and compromise.

As appropriate and applicable to your organization, implement an identity theft prevention program and create or enhance a security strategy & governance committee that includes business partners across the enterprise. Keep formal meeting minutes, log action items, and follow-through. Your peers and those further up the chain will respect and admire your efforts, especially if you're well-organized and humble.

6

Establishing Strong, Strategic Alliances & Business Relationships

Building strong, positive, company-wide relationships benefits All

One cannot emphasize the importance of building strong, strategic, mutually-beneficial relationships with business partners at the organization you work for. Doing so opens a world of opportunity, including additional support for your security-related initiatives, a greater rapport across varying business units, more respect for the Information Security department, and potentially adds new steps on the ladder of your career.

It's most certainly an honor when the Chief Executive, Operating, or Financial Officer of the company, or a similarly high-ranking official, requests your input on the direction the company is headed with respect to security and risk. Likewise, other business leaders, if you've partnered with them on multiple occasions, will eventually want (and need) to know what Information Security thinks and if it endorses the project(s) or initiative(s) at hand.

Consider contract reviews, as an example. Your company should follow a fairly, well-defined process for reviewing contracts with third-party vendors. Subject matter experts (SMEs) from several disciplines should each look over the parameters of proposed vendor agreements and share their input; including changes, additional (contractual) language, etc.

SMEs, at a minimum, should include representatives from your company's internal, otherwise external, legal and audit teams, information security, the risk and compliance, data privacy, and human resources, and accounting/budgeting departments, possibly others. By ensuring each of the appropriate departments are involved in the review and approval of vendor contracts, your company will be way better protected against law suits, data breaches, security and access violations and, instead, acquire more solid insurance coverage, lower risk, and enhance data protection over all.

During the process of reviewing contracts, it behooves you, the strategic Information Security leader, to look for opportunities to support your peers in other departments when they bring up concerns and solutions. Likewise, there may arise times when you should, respectfully, disagree with or add to the suggestions of peers.

Always ensure you come across professionally and respectfully, most notably when your point of view may conflict with that of your peer(s). More often than not, it's how you say something that sets the tone of how it's received; even more than the actual words you speak.

Beyond contract reviews, continually look out for opportunities to partner with other business areas, support their efforts, inject security safeguards (where appropriate), and leverage the bonds you've built to help your department succeed. Keep the momentum going as you interact with other departments and learn how they operate. Eventually, you will have the opportunity to make Information Security a part of every business area's operations.

Certainly, in some spaces, Information Security may play only a minor role or have a minimal influence, which still beats not being involved at all. In other areas, your department will have a much larger presence and end up invited to meetings related to new and existing projects, shifts in the company's direction, operations and structure, and new ventures, including partnerships with other corporations. Strategically leading the Information Security department involves so much more than access control, firewalls, intrusion detection systems, and cloud security.

Granted these, and related facets of information security, are a large part of what you're likely involved with. The point here is that if you're too focused on *your* initiatives and know too little about how the business operates, what changes are occurring, who handles what across each major department, you'll learn about major changes *after* they're decided on and implemented as opposed to when they're brought up.

The former leaves you without input and could place the company at risk, while the latter allows your hand to shape the outcome, ensuring the appropriate security parameters are considered and implemented.

An article in SC Magazine, by Karen Epper Hoffman, further drives home the point of working with and helping the business succeed as a Chief Information Security Officer (CISO). Hoffman writes "once considered the executive most likely to nip a plan in the bud, the Chief Information Security Officer is quickly becoming the person most likely to help make things happen." [5].

Partnering with, assisting, aiding...whatever you want to label it, Information Security leaders will find greater success and career satisfaction when they learn about, align with, and help ensure that their business partners succeed. Business partners, like Internal Audit, need to consider the Information Security department as teammates in helping ensure the company maintains compliance with policies, laws and, in many cases, best practices.

Often, Information Security and other professional leaders view internal, or external, auditors as adversaries seeking to find fault in their respective departments and practices. They feel auditors over-emphasize minor deficiencies and dread working with them.

However, far more benefit will come from working with auditors than against them. Hence, when auditors arrive, look for ways to aid them in their information gathering, be honest and open with them, and work together toward finding appropriate methods to remediate findings.

Providing evidence, such as screenshots, copies of documents, and the like that supports proper security controls exist is key in working well with auditors and thus, scoring high marks on their audit reports. By working with and assisting auditors, you'll find their audit report to executive management likely providing less emphasis on deficiencies and, instead, sharing some healthy changes to better secure the organization. You might even find complimentary language emphasizing the great job Information Security is doing.

Other departments, like legal, loss prevention, risk management, facilities, and physical security, should become like siblings to the Information Security team as these departments often share common goals. Hence, they can and should seamlessly handle employee and incident-related investigations, while partnering with human resources (HR), find and correct issues with policy compliance, highlight and fix safety issues, and ensure compliance with internal policies, as well as the law.

If, for any reason, you find discord in one or several of these areas, work to iron out the differences and ensure a positive, productive relationship emerges and solidifies. Speaking of human resources, Information Security should function as their investigative right-arm, unless the organization employs a different structure for investigations, such as placing that responsibility within the law department, loss prevention, or a similar discipline.

Regardless, you may be called upon to assist with investigations no matter who runs them, so it's best to make it clear you're there to help. If you procure a strong relationship with HR, for example, they will likely include you in investigations they're working on, as appropriate, along with their findings and concerns.

This, in turn, grants you access to details on security-related issues that may aid you in helping to bolster the organization's security posture. For instance, if HR shared with you that two employees accessed, saved, and e-mailed customer records outside the company, you might re-examine your e-mail filter rules to locate and quarantine messages like that to prevent them from leaving the company. Likewise, you may even determine there is a need for a system/server/database monitoring tool to help uncover, if not prevent, fraudulent activity from occurring.

Don't rely too heavily on other departments, like public relations, creative services, marketing & sales, advertising, and others to keep you informed. If you're turned into what's happening within these areas, you'll find yourself involved as the subject matter expert (SME) on several of their projects. Your input can help ensure that agreements with third-party vendors, along with other facets of new and ongoing initiatives, incorporate proper security parameters.

Always mindful to avoid becoming the department of "no," simply examine the details of each project and initiative, share thoughts and concerns tied to reasonable solutions, and assist with additional analysis, review, and even testing, as necessary. You never know who has the ear of the organization's president, board of directors, or other top-level executives.

Imagine them sharing their gratitude (of the Information Security department/leader) with their partners at the top of the organization and what a positive impact that may have on you and your team!

Simply put, the value of partnerships across the entire organization cannot be measured. All too often, professionals simply focus on their own areas, their own niche, instead of the broader, greater good for the organization. Every department has value in an organization.

Otherwise, that department wouldn't exist for very long. Increase the value of Information Security by earning the respect and appreciation of every department you come in contact with. The benefits of doing so will emerge multi-fold, and your boss and others will appreciate knowing they have an amazing team player working for them.

Present timely, pertinent information to executive committee members

After building and maintaining strong, positive working relationships with all departments you interact with, you'll find yourself with a mountain of valuable information. Take time to organize the most pertinent details on paper and request the opportunity to present an Information Security Update to an executive committee, the board of directors, and/or a similar entity within your organization.

Imagine how wise and informed you will look when, during your presentation, you reference the new social media campaign and how it will not only reach thousands or millions of new and existing clients (or customers), but that it will do so in accord with US state and federals laws while embracing secure communications end-to-end.

The executives receiving your presentation will get the impression, rightfully so, that you're involved in the successes of these high-profile projects. Such can only lead to feathers in your cap, as they say, creating (more) job security, potentially higher raises and bonuses, and even stronger relationships with your business partners.

In most cases, executive leaders are "get to the point" types, where too much detail bores them, and too little may lead to awkward questions. When presenting to these leaders, include just enough detail to explain why something is secure or better, more efficient, cost-effective, etc. without drowning them in metrics and examples.

However, have the metrics, examples, and support data at the ready, so you may refer to it if asked. Be prepared for questions like "what are other companies like ours doing in this space?", "where do you research this technology?", and "what makes this the best solution for us?"

Further, avoid painting a picture of doom and gloom, but instead address the fact that there are always new challenges and threats on the horizon, followed by the fact that your organization has tools and resources in place to mitigate these threats and overcome related challenges, unless you're making a case for the purchase of new data security or privacy solutions.

If so, then you'll need to prove where and why the organization is presently deficient, without coming across overly-negative, and share how the proposed solution(s) mitigates risks and better secures the company and its data. Provide an example or two of your organization's technology and consider having an individual or two, possibly on your team, briefly sharing their expertise and experience, then move to the next topic, or conclude your presentation, as appropriate, inviting questions and any other commentary.

Post presentation, plan to provide another update next quarter or later that year. With the support of your boss and possibly several others, presentations to the organization's executives can become a regular occurrence and one that helps ensure you have appropriate funding and are recognized for your involvement in so many areas of accomplishment.

Lastly, make sure your boss sees your presentation before you deliver it. His/her review of your presentation will help you avoid touching on an overly-sensitive topic and may prevent you from surprising your boss when he/she hears you discussed a topic that he or she would have preferred you avoid for political or other reasons, of which you would not have been aware had you not asked.

Summary & Additional Insights

Your eagerness and efforts to assist and develop strong bonds with all departments you interact with, along with sharing timely, pertinent information with executive committees and/or the company's board of directors, will help you become a well-liked, senior leader of

Information Security with job security and a rewarding career ahead of you.

Some additional thoughts: never discount the value of soft skills. Technical, tactical, strategic, and leadership skills are extremely important, yet so are even softer skills, such as those involving negotiation, compromise, likeability, and relationship-building.

Public-speaking is another talent worth adding or improving, along with creating presentations that offer just the right amount of detail and keep the audience's attention. Always gear presentation content to the specific audience versus delivering the same presentation to a highly-technical crowd that you would to an executive board.

Determine what's important to the executive leaders of the organization, particularly the Chief Information Officer (CIO), Chief Financial Officer (CFO), Chief Operating Officer (COO), and, of course, Chief Executive Officer (CEO) or their equivalents, if named differently at the company you work for.

Understanding their needs, you can cater your vision, plans, and actions toward helping key executives meet their goals. There may be other key executives in your organization as well to consider.

Regardless, you should (eventually) present your plans, goals, concerns, and solutions, as mentioned above, to an executive board or committee without including too much detail within your presentation, yet having the detail on-hand, printed or on your laptop or tablet, in order to answer questions effectively. Shooting-from-the-hip is a quick way to "lose face" if you misstate or misquote a fact, figure, or state a thought that comes out differently intended.

Take a deep breath before answering a question, allowing yourself a moment to quickly ponder what you're going to say and how it might be interpreted. Feel free to ask if you can get back to someone on their question as to provide a more-detailed, appropriate answer, then make sure to follow-up rather quickly.

Unfortunately, people in general often notice mistakes more than they notice the great things we do in life and in our jobs. Minimizing mistakes and maximizing your successes helps turn the tide in your favor!

7

Continuous Internal Improvement

Make Learning an Active Part of Your Career

Whether you're already well-established in your career, just starting out, or somewhere in between, periodic self-evaluations of skills, certifications, formal education, and on-going training are vital to your success. The same can be said about the team you manage, where you may want to lead the charge and help determine when your employees need to increase their knowledge, exposure, etc. so that it melds well with their own goals and the needs of the organization.

For now, let's start with you. Do you hold any industry-recognized security certifications, such as the Certified Information Security Manager (CISM) or Certified Information Systems Auditor (CISA) from the Information Systems Audit and Control Association (ISACA), the

Certified Information Systems Security Professional (CISSP) from the International Information Systems Security Certification Consortium (ISC)^2, Security+ from the Computing Technology Industry Association (CompTIA), Certified Information Privacy Professional (CIPP) or Certified Information Privacy Manager (CIPM) from the International Association of Privacy Professionals (IAPP), and/or any of the SysAdmin, Audit, Network, and Security (SANS) certifications?

If so, are they current or has one or two expired or not been maintained? If you don't hold any or hold one that you earned many years ago, consider another relevant certification. Professional certifications distinguish practitioners from taking their careers serious enough to gain the necessary knowledge to earn formal credentials.

On that same vein, do you hold a bachelor's or master's degree in the technology, security, or a similar discipline? If not, you may want to go back to school and, whether degree seeking or not, take some relevant courses.

Education, just like certifications, will never harm you and is a very important piece of your overall skill set. For instance, consider a course on business intelligence, computer forensics, or fraud detection and deterrence. These topics are probably related to your position and can come in quite handy when you are involved with an internal or external investigation or possibly help you uncover employee misbehavior. Taking academic courses shows your boss and others that learning is important to you.

Likely, the company you work for has some form of educational reimbursement. In addition, testing and preparatory materials for professional certification(s) may also be covered by your organization. If only a portion of the costs toward increasing your education are covered by your organization, or even if none are, consider paying out of pocket as the value will far exceed the cost.

At least annually, you should evaluate your skills versus what your position now requires, given duties and responsibilities evolve over time, and new technologies and threats emerge constantly. It would also prove helpful to evaluate what skills are "hot" or in high demand within the security industry.

Take Cloud Computing as an example. It would certainly behoove you to understand how cloud technologies work, what risks exist, methods of securing data in the cloud, alternative solutions, etc. Many companies are *flying* toward "the Cloud" to store their data assets. Are you prepared for a conversation with the Chief Information Officer (CIO) or another executive about the risks of storing personally identifiable information (PII), intellectual property (IP) or other confidential data in a Cloud?

At a minimum, you should comprehend the differences between personal, private, public and hybrid Clouds, along with the risks and rewards of each. For that matter, are employees where you work storing your organization's documents in their own personal Cloud spaces? Is your internet (web) content filter preventing employees from reaching Cloud storage sites or are you allowing the wild west of data storage to lead the company down the path of a potential data breach?

Look for opportunities to learn about new technologies, new risks and threat vectors, and the ways and means to secure and control them. There are countless free webinars available via reputable companies on the internet. There are also many that cost a hundred or several hundred to attend, which are often less vendor-specific and "salesy" yielding more educational content.

The knowledge is available for those willing to take some extra time and reach for it. Make learning an active part of your career. After taking an inventory of your skills, experience, and education, then assessing areas you should increase your exposure in, formulate a plan to incorporate time to learn new competencies so you may apply them appropriately at your organization.

When it comes to the team you manage, you ought to have one-on-one meetings scheduled periodically, such as every 2 or 3 weeks, to assess and discuss how they're doing, how engaged they are with the team's overarching goals, if there are any challenges they're facing, what areas they may need help with, their personal goals, accolades they've received, etc.

During these sessions, planning their personal development is important and shows them you're interested in their success; not just your own. Help each of your direct reports map out personal development plans and, where you're able and its appropriate, provide them with funding for security-related webinars, conferences, etc.

Seek feedback your teammates during this time as well and ensure they know you can come to them with anything, including criticism. Their ideas have value and may collectively reveal new solutions and efficiencies that the entire team, let alone the company, can enjoy.

Join and Participate in Professional Organization Meetings

Next, explore professional organizations related to information security, such as the International Systems Security Association (ISSA), the International Information Systems Security Certification Consortium (ISC)², the Information Systems Audit and Control Association (ISACA), the Institute of Internal Auditors (IIA), the International Association of Privacy Professionals (IAPP), the Federal Bureau of Investigation (FBI) Infragard, and/or the United States Secret Service Electronic Crimes Task Force (ECTF).

There are certainly other great professional organizations as well. You should, at minimum, join several security-related associations and attend their meetings where you'll learn about current crimes affecting businesses, including varying types of fraud, new technologies to mitigate old and current threats, data breach response management, security-auditing techniques, and more.

You'll likely have a story or two to share with your peers, team, and/or boss when you return to the office. You may find yourself interested in participating in one or more of these organization's leadership teams as well.

Not only will attending and participating earn you continuing professional education (CPE) credits for your certification(s), but you'll gain additional exposure amongst peers and may eventually end up speaking on a panel or giving a presentation to one of these groups. In addition, network with your peers in the industry and, once trust/confidentiality is built and confirmed within the group, and you can share stories about the workplace and related security concerns.

Often, peers at other organizations have experienced the same or similar scenarios you brought up and may have some keen insight that helps you deal with issues plaguing your organization or possibly gaining funding and support from upper management toward projects you know the organization desperately needs. Expand your networking circle, via professional organizations, and bring new ideas and solutions into your organization.

Likewise, share your thoughts and advice with other professionals in your field and build an informal, trusted security collective of professional peers. The value of doing so cannot be measured, and you'll thank yourself when you overcome a major security challenge by incorporating some of the suggestions of fellow practitioners.

Likewise, it will feel terrific when a thought you share aids a colleague in solving their security challenge(s). Peer relationships are a valuable and inexpensive resource you can leverage toward learning from and assisting others.

When attending security and related conferences, make sure you network like crazy. You never know who you'll meet, what you'll learn, and how many solutions may land in your lap by simply opening up and talking to fellow security practitioners. Once the conversations are flowing, ideas that never before entered your head can appear and lead to solutions that otherwise never would have been considered.

Keep plenty of business cards on hand and give them out like candy on Halloween, particularly to security professionals in similar roles to yours. Ask if you may contact them if you ever run into a situation at work where their input might help. Likewise, offer them the same by inviting them to call or e-mail you if they need some advice or want to share a scenario with a fellow security professional.

Find and Consider Being a Mentor

Many accomplished leaders attribute a portion of their successes to working with a mentor. If you do not have a mentor, consider looking for someone who will accept you as their mentee. For starters, you ought to ask someone you know quite well; however, that's not a requirement. The selected individual should be in your field or one very similar.

Mentors are phenomenal sounding boards, advice centers, guidance counselors, and career motivators. Hence, you ought to be comfortable sharing virtually anything with your mentor and asking him/her to advise you accordingly.

Also, your mentor should challenge and empower you. It's not uncommon that a mentor will push you past your limits in an effort to help you succeed, manage your career, and grow professionally. If you're not being challenged by your current mentor, let he or she know it and ask that they work with you further. If that doesn't get things moving, consider finding a new mentor.

Regardless, great mentors take pride in helping their mentees succeed and spend ample time and energy doing so. Contrarily, is there someone in or outside of your organization who needs guidance? Consider asking if they'd like you to mentor them. You may even find that someone on your team wants you to mentor them.

While that may seem like a perfectly good idea, in general, your existing relationship of boss to employee is considered too close and often not appropriate for a mentor-mentee relationship. Also, if you have other employees, they may feel that favoritism is occurring as you work on your mentoring responsibilities with your mentee/employee.

It will most likely prove more appropriate if you mentor someone who does not directly report to you. However, use your best judgment. The individual need not work for the same organization, thought there is no harm if he or she does.

Helping others get past their challenges can reveal areas that you too can improve upon. Being a mentor will likely prove rewarding and educational for you and the individual you're guiding. As you share ideas with your mentee, you may come up with the idea that relates to a challenge you're facing.

Hence, it is important to keep a notebook for your mentee within which, you document your mentee's concerns, questions, problem areas, goals and similar, along with ideas and thoughts you come up with. This notebook must be kept private between you and the individual you're mentoring.

Ensure your mentee that what you write down is only for the two of you to go over and reflect on. If your mentee wants copies of what's written in the notebook, oblige them and keep the trust strong between the two of you. Mentoring someone is a rewarding experience and one that mutually benefits both parties in many ways.

If ever you decide to let another individual, such as your boss, someone interviewing you, a friend or family member, know that you're mentoring someone, you need not share the individual's name. In fact, it's best that you ask your mentee if he/she would like your mentoring relationship to be kept private or if they're open to others knowing about it. Whatever they decide, you must abide by.

Summary & Additional Insights

Don't let the busyness of the business prevent you from evaluating your personal plans for continuing education at least annually. Set goals with reasonable timeframes and increase your skillsets and the value you bring to your position.

If you manage a team, encourage your employees to also set goals to increase their knowledge as you lead by example and steer them toward professional development. Incorporate attendance at industry-related professional organization meetings where you, and members of your team, can learn and network with fellow information security professionals, share challenges, and help each other handle issues in the workplace. Also, consider finding a mentor and possibly mentoring someone else. Rewarding experiences await you!

8

Moving from Pilot to Navigator to Governor

Strategically Maneuver Your Career

Unless you've just started your career as an Information Security professional, chances are you're guiding a security program, like a pilot guides or flies a plane, through the organization as a protector of systems, information, assets, etc. with possibly some compliance and policy-related responsibilities. This is terrific and should be maintained, however, it's likely time to expand your footprint.

Enterprise Security, a slightly broader way to describe your role, means covering most of, if not the entire, spectrum of security in your organization. This includes physical security as well, presuming the organization you work for has the appetite for such a combination.

After you've built strategic partnerships across the organization and assisted many different teams with their initiatives, it's time to have a chat with your direct supervisor about broadening your role. You may also need to share your visions of taking on new/additional facets of Information (Enterprise) Security with a few select executives, beyond your boss, as well; proceeding with an ounce of political caution, of course.

You can start by assessing the needs of the company. Where are the weak spots?

I. **Asset Management & Physical Security**

A. Are laptops and other assets often lost and/or stolen?

B. Are employees lax in locking their desks, cabinets, and offices to ensure confidential data remains safe?

C. Are entry and exit points properly secured and monitored?

II. **Risk Management**

A. Are new projects receiving risk evaluations that determine whether or not additional safeguards are needed?

B. Are threats to the success of a project or initiative analyzed and characterized?

C. What vulnerabilities exist within systems, plans, projects, etc., are they documented with solutions to mitigate them, and do they include timelines for completion?

III. ID Provisioning & Deprovisioning

A. Is there a defined process to create access for new employees, change access for employees who switch roles, and remove access for those who leave the organization?

B. Are disabled IDs and accounts that haven't logged on for 30 days or longer audited?

C. Are system and administrative IDs monitored and their passwords changed regularly?

IV. Internal Investigations & Loss Prevention

A. Are your employees' actions monitored to protect the organization against insider threats?

B. Is someone in-house investigating employee malfeasance and fraud?

C. Are abnormal behaviors, such as rogue queries, large record dumps, and unwarranted exploring of network resources, logged, monitored, and alerted on?

The above shares but a few areas that could if not already, fall under your umbrella. After leaning on your partners in the business, those with whom you've built a strong rapport, and after you've examined the direction the business is headed and looked for new projects and teams and in need of security guidance, ask if you can take on some of their security-related work.

Tread lightly, however, as some individuals may feel you're encroaching on their territory. Let them know your hope is to free them up to handle other priorities while you take on tasks that are in line with the security team's (expanding) charter or structure.

Make sure your boss supports this effort before you reach out to other leaders in the business seeking to move some of their work over to your team. If your supervisor is unsupportive, find out why and see if there are other security-related tasks he or she supports your department taking responsibility for.

The goal here is to simply increase your team's ability to support the business, while also opening up a wider career path for yourself. If successful, you'll take on more responsibility and likely reap the rewards down the road, such as a larger team, a promotion, an increase in pay, etc.

As you continue expanding your role navigating the security program throughout the organization, you'll move from "Pilot," which involves an ad-hoc approach toward security, into more of a "Navigator" role, whereby you are more tactical in your methods toward securing the business.

Over time, as your team and responsibilities expand even further, you should move in the direction of a "Governor" role, where you incorporate a strategic vision of Enterprise Security and all its sub-disciplines (investigations, physical security, access management, network security).

At this point in your career, your title may reflect Enterprise Security Director or Vice President, Chief Security Officer, Chief Information Security Officer, or something similar.

Prior job titles, while in a "Pilot" (style) role, consist of Sr. Security Analyst or Lead, Security or Information Security Supervisor or Coordinator, and similar. Likewise, for the "Navigator" role, you'll carry titles like Sr. Security Engineer or Architect, Security or Information Security Manager or Sr. Manager.

Don't get hung up on titles though; many professionals feel their title defines them. It's actually the other way around. You define your title by acquiring long-term vision and strategy, including core business goals, and incorporating them appropriately as your role evolves. Security becomes less separated from the business, as your role matures, and weaves its way into nearly every aspect of the business.

See Diagram 8-1 for more on Information
Security Leadership Roles

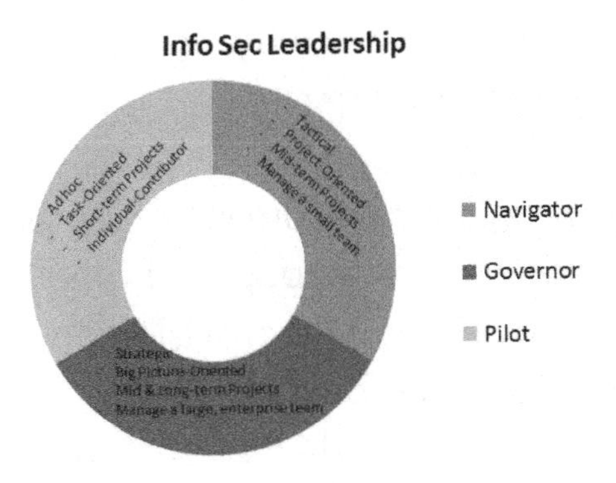

If you want to move from one role to the next, start taking on more projects, thinking mid- and long-term when it comes to initiatives you work on and lead, in and make more strategic decisions. Sometimes, you have to perform as if you're in the role you desire and, after doing so, those around you take notice and help lift you to the next level, be it directly or indirectly.

Consider the following example, an Information Security Sr. Lead, after building a great rapport with whomever he/she comes in contact with, holds several successful project deployments under his/her belt and a Bachelor's degree related to Information Security, plus one or two security certifications, is permitted to hire a Security Analyst reporting to him/her.

Now, a team of two, this Information Security Sr. Lead is primed for a new title, provided he/she continues to excel and delivers projects on-time and on-budget, while looking further down the road for areas he/she can contribute to and possibly "own" as part of his/her team's responsibilities. Sure enough, after some time passes, the Information Security Sr. Lead is granted the new title of Security Manager.

Rather than rest on his/her laurels, he/she pushes forward and takes on the work of a couple of other departments, such as ID Provisioning/Deprovisioning and internal Investigations, and is a constant source of assistance to the Physical Security and Risk Management teams. His/her direct supervisor is aware of his/her long-term goals and the desire to take on more security and related work, thus expanding the security team's footprint.

A few years go by with even greater, successful rapport-building efforts. Now the company's C-Level executives are aware of his/her efforts and invite the (now) Security Manager to occasionally speak at their strategic leadership meetings. His/her security team expands again, and now he/she has several direct reports, including multiple Security Analysts, a Sr. Security Engineer, and possibly a Security Architect.

A new title arrives and the once Information Security Sr. Lead is now the Director of Security for the organization. With such a title, in this example, he/she could potentially request that Physical Security come under his/her umbrella if the timing is right. His/her role continues to expand, nearly every major project involves Information Security, and thus he/she is consistently consulted for security guidance.

The company's security program is not just growing, but blossoming as the organization follows guidance from ISO/IEC (International Organization for Standardization (ISO)/International Electrotechnical Commission), becomes Payment Card Industry (PCI) Data Security Standard (DSS) compliant, and/or acquires a similar security-related designation, depending on the nature of the business.

Also, if the organization does business internationally, it must understand and comply with international regulations, such as the General Data Protection Regulation (GDPR) out of the EU or the Personal Information Protection and Electronic Documents Act (PIPEDA) out of Canada. As the security program of the organization grows and matures, such designations are within reach if the company's leadership supports a world-class program.

Don't be discouraged if they don't, though, for PCI DSS, it's not a matter of wanting to be compliant, it's frankly required to process credit card transactions. With the GDPR, if you have personal data belonging any customers or associates that reside in Europe, you must achieve and maintain compliance.

Failure to do so will prove very costly and potentially tarnish the organization's reputation. There are plenty of other laws and regulations you'll want to explore and need comply with. Start networking, researching, learning, and work with the right team(s) in your organization to prioritize compliance.

Governance, Risk, & Compliance (GRC)

With the expansion of the information security department's responsibilities, an appropriate next step would be to create a Governance, Risk, & Compliance (GRC) Committee with representation from information security, risk management, compliance, legal, information technology, and finance for starters. Over time, you may find the need to invite other departments to attend meetings held by the committee.

The GRC Committee is responsible for discussing IT and Security Controls, new/changes to relevant policies, enterprise risk within projects, initiatives, ventures, etc., and new technologies, as well as challenges the company is facing that, involve risk and/or security. After forming the committee, it is best to create a written charter that summarizes the purpose and goals of the committee and shares the title of each core member.

Next, an inaugural meeting should be scheduled with a well-formed agenda – one that pulls in current concerns highlights new initiatives and the risks they may pose and sets the tone for future committee meetings. Copious notes (minutes) are a must and should be distributed to those in attendance within a day or so of each meeting's conclusion.

This ensures topics are fresh in the minds of committee members and offers them a chance to review and add to the minutes, as needed. The committee will then share or present a report to senior executives, on a regular basis, summarizing its actions, advice, and accomplishments. It's important to note that Governance, Risk, & Compliance (GRC) has several, slightly different interpretations.

You should mold your definition in accordance with your organization, however, a basis for how to define GRC is listed below in Diagram 8-2.

By including the right business unit leaders in a GRC team or committee, you collectively recommend changes to existing initiatives and provide risk ratings to new or revisited projects. You can use and/or adjust the following scale to determine a risk rating, whereby the higher the risk, the more senior-level approval required for it to exist or continue:

		Impact				
		Trivial	Minor	Moderate	Major	Extreme
Probability	Rare	Low	Low	Low	Medium	Medium
	Unlikely	Low	Low	Medium	Medium	Medium
	Moderate	Low	Medium	Medium	Medium	High
	Likely	Medium	Medium	Medium	High	High
	Very likely	Medium	Medium	High	High	High

For example, allowing live (not test) data in a development environment, where that data includes actual individuals' addresses, phone numbers, etc. yields major risk. Thus, a GRC or similar committee would collectively rate the probability that an issue would arise and the level of impact an issue would have on the organization.

A rating of Moderate-Major, which yields a Medium Risk Level, may be appropriate given other factors, such as how many administrators have access to the development data, whether or not each has their own individual log in credentials, how many live data records exist in the system, and how long before test data can, if possible, replace the live data.

Similarly, if an older Oracle database is used on a system with no personally identifiable or confidential data on it, the probability of an issue may be Moderate or Likely, yet the impact to the business if compromised would be Low or Minor. Such a situation would yield a Low-Risk Rating requiring less senior-level approval to continue (using that database) versus the above example of live personal data existing in a development environment.

Summary & Additional Insights

You are in control of the direction your career takes. With determination, strategic decision-making, strong business partnerships, and some patience, you can go from piloting an Information Security program to navigating the direction you and your team take within the organization and eventually govern the entire security process for the company.

During your journey, you should consider forming a Governance, Risk, and Compliance (GRC) Committee that oversees projects, new ventures, initiatives, and operations. The committee will look for risks and ways to mitigate them, ensure compliance with policies and best practices are maintained, and allow security to become embedded within as many projects and practices as appropriate.

As a strong, strategic Information Security leader, focusing on the protection of the organization, its assets (especially data), and associates, while looking ahead at and planning toward the company's long-term success, you'll position yourself and your team at the pinnacle of Enterprise Security governance and make a sizeable impact on the success of your organization.

9

Stay Focused, Vigilant, Increase Spheres of Influence, & Practice Servant Leadership

There's a reason you're a leader, or strive to become one, in Information Security; be it your passion and drive, your willingness to go above and beyond, your iron clad work ethic, and/or natural talent. You recognize that average professionals receive average results, average raises, and average career paths. You desire more and are willing to do what's necessary to achieve it. Hence, you must stay focused, remain vigilant, and go that extra mile, or two, in your efforts to make a difference in and outside of your organization.

Within your organization, you must carve out new paths of involvement and interaction for Information Security. Taking on new tasks, such as ID Provisioning, Investigations, Physical Security, Data Protection, etc. is but one of many channels for you to explore. An open mind and some creativity will go a long way as you learn more about your organization's structure, plans, revenue streams, etc.

Consider the fact that most Information Security departments in an organization are non-revenue generating. This means that they do not make money (directly) for the company, but instead use the funding they receive to provide security and data protection, peace of mind, and prevent financial, as well as reputational, loss. Most certainly, there is nothing wrong with preventing tragedy and saving the company's reputation, as well as preserving its bottom line. In fact, doing so works very well.

However, what if your department could generate some revenue for the company? Would that be worth the CEO and CFO's attention? Not all organizations can enable Information Security to yield income, yet it's still worth trying, provided the organization supports said effort. One method to widen your team and the tasks it performs, while making some money for the company, includes creating a sub-department that provides Information Security consulting for customers.

If structured properly, one to several of your employees could go out to customer sites and advise on, and potentially provide services for, network segregation, access management, data loss prevention, data forensics, web application security, systems hardening...you get the picture. Such services would be appropriately billed to customers and thus generate some additional revenue for the organization.

Of course, specialized agreements, including liability-related statements, etc. would need to be crafted for such engagements. Another means to generate revenue from within Information Security is to host an Information Security conference, whereby vendors and well-known practitioners are invited to advertise and present, for a fee, to other Information Security professionals in the area.

In some cases, professional speakers may charge the organization, yet if the numbers work out, and you also charge a nominal fee for Information Security professionals to attend, while including lunch, for example, then advertise the event accordingly, this could become an annual event for the company, and not only bring in some money, but positively impact the brand.

While the event is advertised, so is your organization, and positive feedback from the conference reflects well on the company's reputation. It would take some planning and likely involve a few upfront costs, however in the end, if structure appropriately, it should generate enough money to make it well worth repeating.

You should partner with local Information Security and similar professional organizations, offering them exposure while they help market the event. They may even provide speakers on timely and popular Information Security topics. You might call it an InfoSec Summit or Conference...some catchy name that offers Continuing Professional Education (CPE) credits. Offering CPEs certainly raise attendance as certified professionals must acquire these credits periodically.

Another method for Information Security to generate revenue, while a bit more challenging, would be to develop a product, process, or unique service, then sell it (or the rights to it). Each of the above suggestions, however, warrants much research, internal discussion, advisement, and the company's willingness to expand the Information Security department's offerings.

Complacency is the Enemy

Irrespective of generating additional revenue, you, as an Information Security leader, must continuously scan the landscape for new opportunities to bring value to your organization. Avoid complacency! So many professionals, in all fields, reach a certain income or achieve a particular title and then feel that they've "made it" and can relax comfortably. Or, an Information Security professional, for example, feels that the program he/she put together is running so well, he/she need not enhance nor change it.

Thoughts like "we've not had a breach (in years)" and "we're so fortified, no one can touch us" breed over-confidence and the Information Security program suffers and grows stale because of it, leaving the company vulnerable to a data breach, malware or virus outbreak, fraud or similar career-limiting calamity.

Technology changes constantly and therefore new threats are always on the horizon. Tools, software, firewalls, network topology...all need attention, tweaking, and periodic updates. Make complacency and laziness your enemies and keep examining ways to expand your Information Security program.

Consider More Than Just Your Career Path's Expansion

While expanding your career is important, the paths you take to get there can vary dramatically. You may want to consider an indirect route if you're not achieving your goals as originally planned. If you have a team, consider promoting your top performers.

A stronger, higher-level team should eventually elevate your role as well. If one or several members on your team consistently excel at their goals, are reliable, have gone back to school and/or earned one or more relevant certifications and developed their soft skills as well, they're most likely ready for a promotion.

Supporting your team members' personal and professional goals is absolutely part of your job. Too many managers (non-leaders) focus solely on their own success and often wonder why they struggle. Helping others, even those not on your team, reach new heights in their career reflects positively on you and can easily aid in your quest to move up the ladder.

This practice is right in line with true Servant Leadership, whereby your service toward others helps with their goals and development. In doing so, you also reach your goals and are rewarded in several ways. This is in complete contrast to what most people focus on; self-serving methods.

Servant Leadership involves several facets that ultimately benefit others first. The strongest and most successful leaders, whether in the field of Information Security or not, practice one or several forms of Servant Leadership. The following model broadly reveals methods you should incorporate into your leadership practices.

Beginning with *Value Associates & Colleagues*, you must genuinely appreciate the hard work and dedication your employees and peers put into their daily tasks, not just projects and initiates. Reward them publicly with praise and a gift now and again to show that you, and the organization, appreciate their efforts and commitment.

For example, during a team meeting, present a gift card and a whole-hearted thanks to one of your employees for the great job they did recertifying associate access to one or several of the company's most critical applications.

Next, *Develop Others* by mentoring or simply supporting your associates' efforts to continue their education via formal classes, training courses, or technical conferences, as well as improving their people skills, such as communication, creating effective presentations, and office diplomacy. Your encouragement goes a long way here too.

To *Build & Maintain Community*, you must foster a comfortable and collaborative workplace for everyone you work with. Help other associates get along, if tension exists, by meeting with them separately to root out any issues or concerns. Help make the workplace a welcome haven for new ideas, suggested improvements, and teambuilding.

Consider a team outing, away from the office, designed around both having fun and working (better) together. Similarly, you can help create community outside the organization by leading within professional organizations. Help create an Information Security community of practitioners who are comfortable enough to share their challenges and pain points with others. Seek advice, as well as offer it.

To *Display Authenticity & Accountability*, you must walk-the-talk. If you mess up, don't do what most do and look for someone or something to blame it on. Step up and openly admit your mistake, share what you learned from it, and then assure your peers and associates that it's okay to make mistakes. We're all human, and things happen. As long as we learn from our errors, progress is achieved.

Consider a situation where you approved a request to open up several ports on the company's firewall for a project, without performing due diligence on what risks this may pose. Next thing you know, some malware made it onto the network. Some managers would look to blame the networking team or the security software not being configured correctly.

Instead, a true Servant Leader does not hide from their error(s) and instead apologizes for not having researched (further) the risks of allowing those particular ports to be opened and thus holds his/herself accountable for the issue that resulted. Next time, you'll certainly ensure you know the risks before approving port changes on the company's firewalls.

Likewise, being "authentic" means leading and presenting yourself consistently to all whom you work and interact with. Make sure you avoid putting on a "face" or front when talking to one person, then changing your demeanor to others.

Associates eventually see through this and detect a lack of authenticity, which leads to trust issues and a lack of respect. Instead, lead with consistency and be yourself no matter who you're dealing with.

Stand up for your associates when they're in the right, but challenged by another associate, versus playing the middle ground and simply trying to keep the peace. Contrarily, if someone is wrong, avoid dodging accountability for you and/or your team and show them that owning up to mistakes bolters integrity.

When you *Provide Leadership*, you guide your team with confidence and enlist their aid and support, set a strong, positive example, hold true to your commitments, and share credit for achievements. Servant Leadership involves more than just having others listen to and follow you. Those around you will want to help you, and thus the organization, succeed and remain protected.

Try to occasionally put yourself in your peers' and colleagues' shoes. Is your leadership style one they (and you, if you were them) appreciate, understand, and willingly follow? Never let your position go to your head.

Instead, remain humble and pleasant, while confident and strong. Put others' needs first while prioritizing the goals of the organization. Your objectives will naturally fit within the over-arching requirements of the company.

As you *Share Leadership Practices*, others around you will become empowered to lead as well. And, as appropriate, they should. You're likely not the only leader around. Leaders need to work together, and some may look to you for guidance. Openly share your methods, feedback, ideas, and style. Similarly, you must remain open to both positive and negative feedback about your leadership practices and adjust your techniques where necessary.

In the end, you want to become an associate that everyone enjoys working with, a leader others confide in, and a supporter of others' success. Your attitude and personality, in tandem to your reliability and proficiency, can make or break your (continued) success as a Servant Leader.

Increase Your Spheres of Influence

Whether you have a team or not, look for ways to increase your spheres of influence. Join committees, request to attend other teams' discussions, whether or not they're directly-related to Information Security, to learn more about the business and invite other key decision-makers to your own meetings on occasion and as appropriate.

Consider asking the marketing teams if you may sit in on a discussion involving social media or a new campaign. Let them know you're there to learn. Also, request one-on-one chats with department leaders to discuss details on projects of interest. For example, learn about the types of data being transferred to and from a new vendor.

Are there any high-risk data types, such as social security number, credit card number, or combinations of other personal data, like name, address, phone number, and/or e-mail address? Your department must be consulted on data transfers like this, unless another team has that responsibility.

If the business is not reaching out to you, you must reach out to them. Information Security cannot thrive without knowing how most of the business operates so it can look for and help prevent potential data breaches, access violations, fraud, etc.

Once you start attending other committee and team meetings, you should gradually share your advice when processes seem to be missing necessary security elements. If you do so in a cordial, professional, and well-intended manner, you may find these same departments asking you to return and share expertise. They certainly do not want their project to create a security issue, yet they also don't want Information Security to stifle their efforts.

Appropriate compromises, idea sharing, and research on other ways to achieve objectives will build a strong(er) partnership between Information Security and its colleagues across the business. These same partnerships yield influence, respect, and occasionally advancement.

Summary & Additional Insights

It's far too easy to allow your passion to fade, find complacency, and feel as if you've done enough to secure your organization. Avoid such temptation and press forward as new threats, exploits, and fraudulent methods emerge constantly. Remain vigilant in your efforts to strengthen the security posture of your organization.

In addition, practice Servant Leadership and help others achieve their goals, work toward common objectives, and avoid simply concentrating on what serves you best. Servant Leaders raise everyone's state of being, help their peers and colleagues excel, and find themselves rewarded while doing so.

Lastly, increase your spheres of influence as you learn about new departments and involve yourself, where appropriate, in their meetings, projects, and initiatives, which may start by introducing yourself to key department heads.

10

Define & Monitor Your Mature Security Architecture & Plan for the Future

---

Once you've crafted a well-oiled machine, with respect to the organization's Information Security architecture, you're ready to involve yourself and your team in more of the business' core strategies, check its pulse and plan for the future.

Defining a Mature Information Security Architecture

How will you know when you've successfully built a mature Information Security architecture (or posture)? For one, data the company wishes to protect will be readily-accessible, available, and backed up with appropriate levels of redundancy. Likewise, systems within the organization will ensure data integrity, e.g., data completeness and accuracy.

Also, the confidentiality of that same data will be maintained, rendering it invisible or unreadable, otherwise inaccessible, to unauthorized individuals. You will have researched and implemented an appropriate mix of technologies involving encryption, tokenization, network segmentation, endpoint protection, data loss prevention...amidst many others...to help ensure data availability, integrity, and confidentiality are preserved.

In addition, you'll manage a suitably-sized team with loyal, skilled security professionals supporting you who genuinely care about the success of the department as well as the organization. You'll create and contribute to well-written and approved policies, which will be reviewed annually and "blessed" by executive management. These policies need "teeth." Hence, consequences for non-compliance are documented, applicable to all associates, and enforced by Human Resources. Otherwise, your written policies are merely suggestions.

Consequences generally begin as verbal warnings, depending on the severity of each policy violation. Written warnings are usually the next phase of discipline, occasionally impacting an associate's performance rating and possibly their merit increase and/or bonus, if such exists at your organization. Repeated policy violations usually lead to suspension and/or termination of employment. Wording, such as, "Individuals who violate this policy are subject to disciplinary actions up to and including termination of employment" should appear within each policy.

You'll have an Information Security Awareness Campaign, which includes far more than annual security training. An Information Security Awareness Campaign also contains security posters in every office break room and in other common areas, such as near printers, fax machines, copiers, etc. These posters share important tips and remind associates to "Treat your password like your toothbrush...don't share it!" and "Lock your computer and desk drawers when you step away or leave for the day."

Plus, an Information Security Awareness Campaign generates quarterly newsletters and/or monthly articles that explain, for example, what phishing attempts are all about, how to spot and handle them and how they can harm individuals and organizations. Other such topics touch on what to do when an event or incident occurs, what ransomware does and ways to protect yourself from it, the importance of not allowing associates to tail-gate you while walking into the building, etc.

On that note, each associate needs to use their badge to gain access. How do associates know that the familiar-looking individual they just held the door for, who thereby just avoided the need to swipe a badge, wasn't let go or fired a day or so prior and hasn't returned to cause problems?

Lunch-n-learn sessions a few times a year, where a member or two of the Information Security department presents a topic, in person, to associates who sign-up to learn more about safe computing and internet browsing or how to recognize and treat confidential, sensitive and personally identifiable information.

Such presentations can also be given to specific departments on a rotating basis and may be delivered online as well. There are many other creative ways to procure a strong Information Security Awareness Campaign and plenty of topics to cover.

A mature Information Security architecture certainly does not stop there. You and members of your team should, by this point, receive invitations to nearly all major meetings to listen-in and share the voice of security, pointing out concerns, highlighting potential vulnerabilities, and offering alternative solutions to keep the business moving forward.

You should find yourself consistently leading and participating in security-related committees, garnering support from major players in the business and assisting them with their priorities. Try to add value to the organization, particularly its core business, where it makes sense, provided your primary objectives, like maintaining data availability, integrity, and confidentiality, are upheld. Imagine the business is opening up an office overseas to increase its sales footprint.

On the surface, a novice Information Security professional may think this overseas expansion does not involve them. While that could be the case, it's rather unlikely. An astute Information Security leader would inquire about the details of this expansion, request information on types of data that will be transmitted to/from and stored in this new office abroad and find out the types of physical security existing there, for starters. Will confidential data be kept in locked storage on-site? Is there a plan in place to effectively backup data?

Policies and standard operating procedures (SOPs) should exist to share with associates at this location who will eventually receive an audit to ensure they're complying. Other items to investigate include whether actual associates will work in this location and/or if (some) temporary, contracting, or outsourced staff will reside there? Are associates at this location given the same new hire training as those in the organization's other locations? The same goes for on-going security training.

Information Security, as a team, should not wait for the organization to invite their input. Be proactive and ask that the business to include your team, or at least you, in discussions involving business decisions, not just those that directly relate to Information Security. There are plenty of indirect Information Security connections to business activities, several of which business decision-makers will not see or may even choose to ignore.

The strong, strategic Information Security leader stays involved with the organization's business activities, asks questions, takes notes and knows when and how to involve his/her team in order to maintain a strong security posture. That said, some business strategies are kept "close to the vest" by the executive team and if you receive push-back when trying to involve yourself in a particular business discussion, accept this decision and gently revisit it down the road.

Your timing can be as important as the actions you take. By now, you (should) have formed a fortified, security architecture the company relies on and, it is at this point, that you can start to review and tweak said architecture and then possibly expand it further.

What's Next?

It's likely time that you, the Information Security leader assess, for yourself, the organization's health, both financially and strategically. Are top executives making rational, wise, and prudent decisions that improve, or at least maintain, the company's brand status, increasing sales and keeping pace with, if not excelling ahead of, its competition? While you may not have all the insight necessary to know these answers, you should keep any eye out for signs as to whether the company's health is on stable, on the rise, or heading South.

For instance, are top executives communicating with upper management and other leaders about the direction the company is taking? Have they always communicated, via a newsletter or town-hall meetings? Have those communications diminished in frequency? Do you feel that something just isn't right? Have several leaders recently left the company?

Are there signs or discussions about merging with another company or a possible sale to a competitor? Is there a sense of uneasiness felt by many employees? Have benefits changed dramatically, such as a significant increase in the cost to each associate for healthcare?

Have the organization's contribution levels (aka employee match) for 401K plans gone down or been suspended, and, if the latter, has this occurred for more once? Have bonus amounts or percentages, if offered, declined more so than in past years?

There are a myriad of signs that point to an organization's difficulty maintaining viability. Whether such signs are starting to emerge or not, they could down the road, and therefore, the truly strategic Information Security leader has a *Plan B*.

As difficult as it may be to consider the thought of leaving the organization you've worked so hard for and helped fortify against threats and risks, the fact is: crap happens! Hopefully, it won't happen to you yet, like your car insurance plan's tire, gas, towing, and loaner vehicle support, having the means to keep you and your career safe will prove comforting and rewarding should tragedy strike.

Begin with your resume. Is it current? Have you documented your recent accomplishments -- those achieved in and outside your organization with the dates they occurred and their significance? Do you have a network of recruiters with whom you can easily get in touch or who reach out to you when Information Security opportunities emerge? Do you have an updated account on popular job sites like careerbuilder.com, dice.com, monster.com, indeed.com, etc.? Have you researched companies near where you live, or where you'd like to move, that you could see yourself working in happily and successfully?

There is no harm knowing what opportunities are out there, what they pay, and what skills are sought after most. You may even want to grab a book on interviewing, if you've not had one in a while, and go through the typical questions asked on interviews, particularly those that might otherwise catch you off guard. A wise and strategic Information Security leader explores the above avenues and other means of securing his/her future.

Returning to and enhancing Plan A

Hopefully, you will not need to invoke your Plan B; however, that does not minimize its importance. After ensuring your resume is up-to-date and knowing what steps to take if you, or the company you work for, decide to part ways, it's time to return to Plan A -- that is, governing versus more tactically-managing, the Information Security program while making minor changes as necessary.

Likewise, you're now (more) comfortable approaching executive management or at least the individual(s) you report to, about Information Security's involvement in business strategies, new ventures, etc.

If you have not been promoted appropriately, given your efforts and the health of the company, now seems like a ripe time to put together a list of your accomplishments, which you've already tackled as part of your Plan B, along with their positive impact on the organization and any additional kudos for you and your team, such as certification achievements or educational degrees earned. After creating this list, re-write it in the most-suitable format for your immediate supervisor.

For instance, if your immediate supervisor is a visual person, you may want to include a graph or two depicting where the company was several years' prior with respect to its Information Security posture, likely low, and where it resides currently as a strong, Information Security foundation within the organization. If your immediate supervisor is detail-oriented, include specific examples of your achievements with approximate start and completion dates, positive impact(s) to the business, etc.

If your immediate supervisor is more of a "bottom line" individual, where just the facts and fewer details are preferred, then a high-level, short, bulleted-list of achievements is likely all you need to present to him/her. Regardless of which method you present your achievements in, include a written (typed) request for a promotion.

Why written?

A written request carries with it a level of seriousness versus verbally asking, which comes across as far more informal. Imagine if you verbally asked for a promotion and your immediate supervisor did not take you seriously, possibly even thought you were joking? This could happen if you ask at the wrong time, for instance, right after you learned that budget-tightening is a priority for the entire company.

Still, timing aside, a formal, written request for promotion coupled to your list of achievements has a better chance of success in most cases than a simple, verbal ask. Just make sure you really know as much as you can on the status of the company's financial and overall health before you present your promotion request and be prepared for the possibility that your promotion may not happen right away.

It's better to hear "I agree that your request for a promotion is warranted and it is under consideration," or something similar to that, than "I'm sorry, we just cannot promote you right now." Even the latter statement may not be so horrible if you politely inquire, to your immediate supervisor, when such a promotion might actually be warranted and fulfilled…

Request feedback from your immediate supervisor if you do not receive a green light on your promotion. Ask "what (additional) steps shall I take in order to reach the point where the organization will raise me to the next level?" If the feedback you receive appears positive and you feel you can achieve the additional goal(s) your supervisor set, start working on them.

Contrarily, if the response you receive is not favorable toward a promotion and you do not feel staying with the organization remains in your best interests, after thinking about it for several days, you may determine it is time to move on and reach the next stage of your career in a different organization.

On a side note, there is value in discussing your path of promotion with your immediate supervisor prior to reaching all or most of the goals you've set. If you can breach this topic with your immediate supervisor somewhere in the middle of your quest to create a mature Information Security architecture, such as a few years into your employment and/or after many, but not most or all, key Information Security milestones have been reached, you can and should incorporate your immediate supervisor's goals for you toward promotion into your strategic plan.

Several years after that, for example, when your own goals and those set by your immediate supervisor toward your promotion are reached, you can show he/she that you've not only significantly strengthened the organization's Information Security posture, but that you've also taken all the necessary steps you, and he/she originally outlined for you to reach the next level in your career. This does not guarantee you will receive the promotion or level you desire within your organization.

However, regardless of the outcome, you can at least take pride in the fact that you achieved all or most of what was required, significantly improved the organization's Information Security program and shared your successes with those you report to.

Summary & Additional Insights

As your Information Security program matures within the organization and you've taken on more of a governance-based role, review your and your team's accomplishments, major milestones achieved, and assess the health of the company, along with your own journey toward promotion, whether that path keeps you working at your current organization or leads you toward another.

11

Final Thoughts

You're now (more) prepared to take on several new challenges, while reviewing existing strategic priorities--those specific to your department and to the organization--and leading your team toward greater responsibility, thus enhancing your company's information (or cyber-) security program and hopefully bolstering your career potential.

Data Protection & Management are a Must

Data, particularly personal and company confidential, are the lifeblood of most, if not all, organizations. It's crucial to learn where data resides within your organization and the value (classification) each set of information holds.

Your applications, databases, systems, off-site and cloud storage, file transfers (internal and external), filing cabinets and desk drawers (both locked and unlocked), local hard drives, portable media, bring your own devices (BYODs) and technologies, internet of (every-) things, etc. may have information (data) on them or connect to systems that do and, if compromised, could bring forth costly fines, public embarrassment, weakened stock values, loss of jobs, and organizational shutdown.

You cannot achieve worthy data protection and management alone or with one simple tool or technology. If your company has a Privacy Officer, a partnership with this individual will serve you both well. If your organization does not have a well-defined privacy role, perhaps you can, in addition to all the other great things you're working on, explore, or recruit others to consider, creating such a role.

A Privacy Officer should not necessary report to or within the same area as Information Security and, arguably, it should be completely separate. Regardless, having someone dedicated to reviewing and classifying data, while keeping up with requirements, such as laws and regulations, around protecting information can make an immeasurable difference.

Just as you partner with other areas of the business, so should you partner with the individual(s) responsible for data privacy, along with the individual(s) responsible for physical security. Data protection and management is a topic that could consume its own book, yet it's briefly mentioned here to get you thinking about how the organization presently protects its important information and if enhancing efforts around such makes sense.

No organization is every truly secure, however if you can look yourself in the mirror and earnestly say "we (you and your team) did all we could to protect the organization from harm given what was available to us, in the way of budget and support, and what was within our department's scope and control," should something tragic happen, such as a major data breach, fraud, insider malfeasance, or similar, your conscience and that of your team, should remain clear. Blaming each other or yourself will not change anything and is more than likely far from appropriate.

Practice professional skepticism and teach your team and peers to do the same. I live by the words "you're most vulnerable the moment you think you're safe," which drives me never to stop learning or let my guard down while trusting only what's verified.

Thank you for reading what's taken me many years to compile and transfer from my mind to these pages. I wish you boundless success and passion around information security and data protection, while keeping others, along with their information, protected.

External References Cited

Disclaimer: All statements in this book, unless cited, are based strictly on my own experiences, observations, education, and opinions and thus, are not representative of any company I work for or with.

[1] Grossman, Steven. "Chief Information Security Officers Should be Reporting to Chief Risk Officers." *SecurityWeek*, September 15, 2016. www.securityweek.com/chief-information-security-officers-should-be-reporting-chief-risk-officers

[2] "World's Biggest Data Breaches." *Information is Beautiful.* www.informationisbeautiful.net/visualizations/worlds-biggest-data-breaches-hacks

[3] Carson, Angelique. "If Nine of 10 Employees Knowingly Breach Policy, How Is Privacy Possible?" *International Association of Privacy Professionals (IAPP)*, June 25, 2013. iapp.org/news/a/if-nine-of-10-employees-knowingly-breach-policy-how-is-privacy-possible

[4] "Red Flags Rule." *Federal Trade Commission.* www.ftc.gov/tips-advice/business-center/privacy-and-security/red-flags-rule

[5] Hoffman, Karen Epper. "CISO: The Great Enabler?" *SC Magazine*, January 2, 2014. www.scmagazine.com/ciso-the-great-enabler/article/540104

Note: Links to online references are subject to change without notice by the companies who own the sites and content on which they are stored.

Made in the USA
Columbia, SC
26 June 2020

12164916R00085